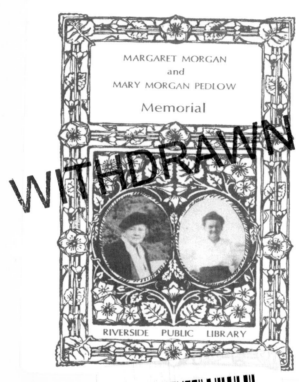

Praise for

THE FEASTS

"Cardinal Wuerl and Aquilina show us the transformative spiritual power in the Church's original and most ancient feasts. This is a book to be prayed with and meditated on. Because when we understand the meaning of the Church's liturgical feasts, we know better the great dignity and destiny we have as children of God."

—Most Reverend José Gomez, archbishop of Los Angeles

"In this highly approachable volume, coauthors Cardinal Donald Wuerl and Mike Aquilina have combined sound research with pastoral sensitivity to take readers on a journey of discovery and inspiration through the Church's liturgical year. Beginning with the fundamental question of why the Church has always celebrated the Eucharist on Sundays, all the way to the origins of feasts of more recent vintage, such as Divine Mercy Sunday, this fine work reminds us that the feasts and seasons we celebrate are not just arbitrary events. Rather, we discover how the Church year is the Church's time-honored way of inviting present-day Christians to learn about, be challenged by, and find hope for the future through the unfolding of the Paschal Mystery in time and the witness of all the saints, upon whom 'we rely for unfailing help' *(quotation from Eucharistic Prayer III)*."

—Archbishop of Louisville Joseph E. Kurtz, president, United States Conference of Catholic Bishops

"This gracefully written book will serve not only as a splendid explanation of the Church's feasts and solemnities but also as an illuminating introduction to the faith itself. Mike Aquilina and Cardinal Wuerl have once again shown their prowess as champions of the new evangelization."

—Robert Barron, author of *Catholicism*

"We have to weigh every opportunity and know the times, says the early martyr Saint Ignatius of Antioch. He encouraged the Christian communities to meet more regularly for the Eucharist. The book *The Feasts: How the Church Year Forms Us as Catholics* is a thorough and very readable guide through the Church's feast days, beginning with Sunday, the Lord's Day! The book invites us to be formed in a genuine Catholic identity and ethos through these beautiful and significant celebrations of our liturgical calendar. Cardinal Wuerl and Mike Aquilina help us to weigh every opportunity for witness to Jesus. The authors show us how the feast days become a connatural way to learn the faith so that we will be intelligent and credible witnesses for the faith."

—Cardinal Daniel DiNardo, archbishop of Galveston-Houston

"Catholics are a people of celebration. More than anything else—we celebrate! *The Feasts* is a fabulous book that will teach you the what, when, where, how, and why of the celebrations that are at the center of our incredible faith. The genius of Catholicism is all around, but often it goes unnoticed. The Church year is full of celebrations—feasts— and they seek to remind us of what matters most. Enjoy this book. It will help you to celebrate in new and profound ways."

—Matthew Kelly, founder of DynamicCatholic.com and author of *Rediscover Catholicism*

"This book delighted my heart! In a style that is simple and gracious, Cardinal Donald Wuerl and Mike Aquilina have brought the extraordinary from the ordinary in *The Feasts*. They bring through the ordinary things of time, calendars, and feast days the timeless things of God through the Incarnation of the Word into our needy world in Jesus Christ. They remind us of the stunning divine realities behind the human calendars and feast days we often take for granted. This sense of bringing the sacred through the secular is a most timely message we often take for granted."

—John Michael Talbot, author of *The Ancient Path*

THE
FEASTS

How the Church Year Forms Us as Catholics

Cardinal Donald Wuerl
and Mike Aquilina

IMAGE

New York

Published in the United States by Image, an imprint of the
Crown Publishing Group, a division of Random House LLC, New York,
a Penguin Random House Company.
www.crownpublishing.com
IMAGE is a registered trademark and the "I" colophon is a trademark of
Random House LLC.

All photos are provided courtesy of the *Catholic Standard,* the official newspaper of
the Archdiocese of Washington, D.C. Photographers are Michael Hoyt,
Rafael Crisostomo, and Leslie Kossoff.

Library of Congress Cataloging-in-Publication Data is available upon request.

ISBN 978-0-8041-3992-2
eBook ISBN 978-0-8041-3993-9

PRINTED IN THE UNITED STATES OF AMERICA

Book design by Ellen Cipiano
Cover design by Jessie Sayward Bright
Cover photograph by Alamy Images

1   3   5   7   9   10   8   6   4   2

First Edition

CONTENTS

Acknowledgments

All photos are provided courtesy of the *Catholic Standard,* the official newspaper of the Archdiocese of Washington, D.C. Photographers are Michael Hoyt, Rafael Crisostomo, and Leslie Kossoff.

Foreword

Most Reverend José Gomez
Archbishop of Los Angeles

Lex orandi, lex credendi.

In the Church's ancient formula, we pray what we believe. And what we pray changes us into what we believe.

We are made in the image of God and given the vocation to be transformed into the image of Jesus Christ. This beautiful promise of our faith shapes the direction of our Christian lives.

Little by little and day by day, we are being changed into his likeness, Saint Paul said. What we will become is not yet clear, Saint John added. But we know that one day we shall be like Jesus.

This transformation is taking place quietly through our participation in the divine liturgy as it unfolds in the rhythms and cycles of the Church's liturgical year—especially in the great feasts that remember the mysteries of Christ's incarnation, Passover, resurrection, ascension, and the sending of his Holy Spirit.

In celebrating this yearly cycle of feasts, we enter into those sacred mysteries, joining our lives to his life.

The Church's liturgy sanctifies time. In the liturgy, God's kingdom comes and enters into our time and place. Each of our lives—and the history of nations—becomes a part of the salvation history that God has been working out since before the foundation of the world.

That's what this fine book is all about. Cardinal Donald Wuerl and Mike Aquilina have recovered this ancient truth—that our Christian worship is meant to be both formative and transformative.

This is an important recovery in this era of globalization and the increasing secularization of society.

Over the centuries and still today, the Church's eucharistic liturgy and her great liturgical feasts have created cultures and shaped identities. The liturgy has inspired some of history's most exalted achievements in art, architecture, music, drama, and literature.

Through the liturgy, the seeds of Gospel have been sown in every culture. And from every cultural soil these seeds have borne rich fruit—in songs and customs, patron saints, pious devotions, and feast days.

Where I live, in Los Angeles, our Catholic culture is expressed in more than forty languages and in popular piety that is drawn from peoples of every continent and more than sixty nations. Our Native American brothers and sisters honor Saint Kateri Tekakwitha. Our Peruvian neighbors celebrate El Señor de los Milagros, "Our Lord of the Miracles." Filipino Catholics pray Simbáng Gabi, a series of nine Masses dedicated to the Blessed Mother on December 16–24. Our Hispanics venerate

Our Lady of Guadalupe and celebrate Christmas Eve with the beautiful Posadas processions.

All of these devotions and popular expressions of faith make up our common family heritage as Catholics. To be Catholic means we can pray in every language and express our faith in countless regional and ethnic traditions. We belong to one family of God drawn from peoples of all nations and cultures. And we are heirs to the authentic Catholic traditions of every culture. What a beautiful blessing this is!

In our times, the Church is called to a new evangelization of culture—to the creation of a "new world," rooted in the transforming power of the sacred liturgy.

Despite the widespread secularization of our societies, we can see that millions of people are hungry for God. They long to make contact with him. They long to know his love and power in their lives. They are searching for spiritualities that will bring them holiness and wholeness and communion with God and other people.

With our rich treasury of Catholic spiritualities, drawn from the Gospel's inculturation in "every nation under heaven," we possess powerful resources for this new evangelization of our culture. Our traditions of popular piety become a part of the good news that the Church is called to bring to the men and women of our world today.

Cardinal Wuerl and Aquilina remind us that all true popular religiosity is rooted in the Eucharist we celebrate every Sunday, the Lord's Day. Sunday is the primordial feast, the remembrance of the day of his resurrection. And from our worship on the Lord's Day, all of the Church's great feasts flow.

Cardinal Wuerl and Aquilina show us the transformative

spiritual power in the Church's original and most ancient feasts. This is a book to be prayed with and meditated on. Because when we understand the meaning of the Church's liturgical feasts, we know better the great dignity and destiny we have as children of God. Following the Church's annual liturgical cycle of feasts, we enter ever more deeply into Christ's mysteries. Our love for him grows, and we gradually come to a deeper understanding of the heart and the mind of Christ. Through our encounter with his mysteries, we are refashioned in his divine image.

In this way, the Church's liturgical year forms and transforms us, through all the days of our lives. And through us—through the witness of our Christian lives in our homes, at work, and in our communities—our culture is being renewed one heart at a time. Our lives become more and more a participation in the great feast of the Eucharist, and a new world is being created in the image of God's loving plan of salvation.

Preface

Father Peter John Cameron, OP
Editor in Chief, Magnificat

His Eminence Cardinal Donald Wuerl and Mike Aquilina have given the Church a great gift of love in the publication of their book *The Feasts: How the Church Year Forms Us as Catholics.*

Where would we be without the feast days of the Church, like the chief feasts of Easter, Pentecost, and Christmas, all the way down to the optional memorials of lesser-known saints whose particular sanctity magnifies the Church's holiness?

As the authors tell us, "When we celebrate the feast days, we are living life to the full, because we are fulfilling a deep need in human nature. God made us to require rest—but, more fundamentally, to desire joy. Still more than that, we want to have a reason for joy." What is the reason for our joy in the feasts we celebrate?

Within weeks of his election to the throne of Saint Peter, Pope Francis began his call for a "culture of encounter." For

example, at World Youth Day in Brazil in July of 2013, Pope
Francis urged, "Be servants of communion and of the culture of
encounter! I would like you to be almost obsessed about this."
Elsewhere he says, "Go out, go out! . . . Because faith is an encounter with Jesus, and we must do what Jesus does: encounter
others."

The Holy Father reminds us what lies at the core of Christian encounter: that Jesus *feasts* with sinners. In his morning
meditation of July 5, 2013, Pope Francis said, "[This] is the
contradiction of the celebration of God: the Lord feasts with
sinners." "It is the memory of mercy and of that celebration that
gives [the followers of Christ] the strength 'to go forward.'"
And this, the pope insists, must be remembered forever.

That "remembering" comprises the liturgical life of the
Church, especially in the celebration of her feasts, both major
and minor. Each liturgical feast that we observe begins with the
memory that God himself in the Person of his Son has deigned
to feast with us unworthy sinners. Every liturgical celebration of
a feast, then, is a call to humility and to true priorities—to what
really matters in life.

Pope Benedict XVI, when he was teaching and writing theology as Joseph Ratzinger, often turned his attention to the
subject of the liturgical feast. He offers three key insights to the
feasts that help us in our own reflection.

First, Cardinal Ratzinger emphasizes that *in faith time is measured by the acts of God,* especially the two great events of the
birth and the resurrection of the Lord. He explains, in the book
Seeking God's Face, that "Christian feasts are based on our in-
sight into these acts of God. . . . The constant return of these
feasts is qualitatively quite different from the endless repetition
of the year from the first day to the last. It is not an eternally

repeated cycle, but the expression of God's inexhaustible love, of which we are made aware by an act of memory."[1]

The authors underscore this fact when they point out that "the feasts themselves are the primary means by which Christians have handed on the faith. . . . The feasts are a teaching, and they teach in a God-like way. . . . A feast teaches by sharing love."

Second, *the Christian feasts reveal the meaning of life.* In the book *Dogma and Preaching,* Cardinal Ratzinger says this:

A Christian feast . . . means that the human person leaves the world of calculation and determinisms in which everyday life snares him, and that he focuses his being on the primal source of his existence. It means that for the moment he is freed from the stern logic of the struggle for existence and looks beyond his own narrow world to the totality of things. It means that he allows himself to be comforted, allows his conscience to be moved by the love he finds in the God who has become a child, and that in doing so he becomes freer, richer, purer. If we were to try celebrating in this fashion, would not a sigh of relief pass across the world? Would such a feast not bring hope to the oppressed and be a clarion call to the forgetful folk who are aware only of themselves?[2]

The authors accentuate this as well: "The feasts form us. They help to make us and remake us according to the pattern of the life of Jesus Christ." We live for the mystery according to the Church's liturgical mysteries.

1 Joseph Ratzinger, *Seeking God's Face* (Chicago, IL: Franciscan Herald Press, 1982), 11.
2 Joseph Ratzinger, *Dogma and Preaching: Applying Christian Doctrine to Daily Life* (San Francisco: Ignatius Press, 2005), 345.

And finally, *the feast is a response to death.* Ratzinger observes that the basis for every feast is joy, but genuine joy is possible, as he explains in *The Feast of Faith,* only "if there is an answer to death":

> The feast presupposes joy, but this is only possible if it is able to face up to death. . . . [T]he feast . . . attempts to answer the question of death by establishing a connection with the universal vital power of the cosmos. . . . The freedom with which we are concerned in the Christian feast—the feast of the Eucharist—is the liberation of the world and ourselves from death. Only this can make us free, enabling us to accept truth and to love one another in truth.[3]

Maybe this is why "feast" is surely one of the happiest words in the English language. For the promise of a feast assures us that someone loves us and wants us and has prepared something wonderful for us; that the experience of feasting somehow opens us to the ultimate meaning and goal of life (see Isaiah 25:6); and that the memory of such shared friendship and celebration portends a future endowed with similar delights.

I know that the nearly five hundred thousand readers of *Magnificat* will welcome and rejoice in this prayerful aid to living the Church's feasts. May the publication of this book be the cause of evermore-worthy worship of God throughout the world. And may that worship move us to go out to feast with fellow sinners so as to bring forth a thriving Gospel culture of encounter.

---

3 Joseph Ratzinger, *The Feast of Faith: Approaches to a Theology of the Liturgy* (San Francisco: Ignatius Press, 1986), 64–65.

THE
FEASTS

Introduction

Satisfy us in the morning with thy steadfast love,
that we may rejoice and be glad all our days.
—Psalm 90:14

CALENDARS FORM US. Calendars help to define us as the people we are.

As small children, we count the days till Christmas, the days till summer vacation, the days till school begins. Each time span seems to track certain feelings, of excited anticipation or dread.

We cannot have a civilization or a culture unless we have some rudimentary calendar—so that we can set our hopes on future days and remember the past with some precision. People who live by their fishing live by their knowledge of the tides, which follow the phases of the moon. Farmers depend on the yearly cycle of seasons.

We take our calendars for granted. But they are among the most marvelous technologies human beings have developed. They are based on data gathered over millennia. They seem self-evident to us, but they are only possible because of the painstaking efforts by many generations of our ancestors.

The lunar cycle is slightly irregular, and the solar year cannot be measured in full days. The calendar we have today was developed to take these and other complications into consideration—and reconcile them by periodic corrections. We make up for differences by observing leap years. Once in the past two thousand years, our governmental authorities ground time to a halt in order to make massive corrections to the calendar—so that it could more accurately line up our seasons with our commercial activity and our religious feasts. That reform took place in 1582, and it was initiated by Pope Gregory XIII. It produced the calendar that most of the world follows today.

Christian life revolves around the calendar that Christians share. The calendar and its feasts remind us who we are. If we want to know ourselves, it is important for us to imagine how this works—how the feasts form us, what they teach us, how they guide and direct our emotions, our thoughts, and our spiritual growth.

Both authors of this book were raised in homes that lived by the Christian calendar. So the feasts have been forming us since we were infants. In the chapters of this book we have gathered doctrinal and historical information about the feasts, because facts are the solid foundation of understanding. But we have also included in the chapters impressions, observations, and memories. It is probably impossible—and anyway unhelpful—for Christian authors to try to teach the feasts in a detached and distant way.

Nevertheless, the foundation must be the facts. To an outsider, the Christian feasts and seasons appear to be a riot of color, custom, cuisine, and music. The feasts affect our diet and our demeanor. For clergy, they affect wardrobe as well. A Friday in Lent has its own unique tastes and sounds and feelings, as does Christmas, as does Easter, as do Pentecost and All Saints' Day and Saint Patrick's Day.

All the feasts are celebrations of Jesus Christ. They begin with the mysteries of his divine and human life. They are rich because his life represents the fullness of creation and redemption.

Because we are human we cannot help but celebrate feasts. It is our nature to remember significant days and celebrate them with other people. We do not permit ourselves to forget anniversaries. We dare not forget the birthday of that special someone in our lives—whether it is a parent, a spouse, a child, or a friend. Because we are human, and because our companions are human, we remember the days and we celebrate.

The Church calendar is a standard medium for the expression of the profound loves at the center of our lives—our love for God and for our family, for our Church and our community. To be Catholic is to have a faith that fills us, body and soul, senses and spirit. To be Catholic is to have a faith that marks our hours, counts our days, and measures our months and seasons.

Keeping the feasts is part of our commitment to live as a child of God. At minimum, we must remember the Lord's Day and keep it holy. But people in love rarely settle for doing the minimum. Love is something we want to celebrate lavishly—and because we love Christ we need to celebrate him and the life of his Church generously.

If fishing villages grow richer from their mastery of the lunar calendar, and if farmers profit from their knowledge of the solar calendar, so much more do Christians benefit spiritually when we understand the Christian calendar—when we've come to know "the reason for the season."

The feasts form us. They help to make us and remake us according to the pattern of the life of Jesus Christ. We number our days as we walk in his footsteps, from his birth to his baptism, from his passion to his resurrection, from his ascension to his sending of the Spirit to make us saints. We do this faithfully every year, and it defines us.

Music makes the meaning of each feast clear and memorable.

We conceived this book as a companion to the two other books we have written together: *The Mass: The Glory, the Mystery, the Tradition* and *The Church: Unlocking the Secrets to the Places Catholics Call Home*. In these books we asked readers to join us in taking a fresh look at the things most familiar to us as Catholics, our principal act of worship and our places of worship. We did not write the three books to be read in sequence. They complement one another, but none of the three depends upon information you'll find only in the others.

This book, like the others, provides an opportunity to look closely at something many of us have known for a very long time. Catholics love to celebrate the feasts, but often passively. The time rolls around each year, and we show up because we have an obligation to do so. And participating brings us joy. But our joy could be far greater if we celebrated with understanding.

So we will begin our study with introductory material about the Christian calendar and the ways we celebrate. We'll look briefly at its origins and development through the centuries. We'll also examine the biblical foundations and general doctrine related to our feasts. With our principles and terminology in place, in the chapters that follow we'll go on to look at the Church's individual major (and some minor) feasts and seasons.

Your authors are Catholics of the Latin Rite, so we refer to the feasts as they are celebrated in our particular tradition. It is a tradition we share with the majority of the Catholics in the United States and indeed the world. One of us is a cardinal-archbishop, and the other is a layman, husband, and father. Thus we often find ourselves playing different roles in the liturgical celebration of the feasts. We hope our differing but complementary experiences will make for a richer discussion of a very rich subject.

The feasts are to time what churches are to space. They are moments we mark off as sacred. They are moments of special grace for our prayer and our common life as a family—a Church.

CHAPTER 1

Where the Feasts Begin

This is the day which the Lord has made;
let us rejoice and be glad in it.
—Psalm 118:24

IF YOU GET OUT MUCH, you've probably seen at least one church signboard with this message: *Seven days without worship make one weak.*

Puns may be the lowest form of humor, but this one manages, rather compactly, to express several profound truths about religion, time, and human nature.

It is natural for us to divide time.

It is human to dedicate time to a transcendent purpose—to mark it off as holy.

It is natural, moreover, for us to link human flourishing with spiritual progress—and to connect spiritual progress, necessarily, with the passage of time. Spiritual change, like any change, is movement from one state to another. And such sequences are what we describe and measure whenever we speak of time.

That common signboard sums up the truths that are at the beginning of all biblical religion. When Christians and Jews tell their story, it starts this way:

> In the beginning God created the heavens and the earth. . . . And God said, "Let there be lights in the firmament of the heavens to separate the day from the night; and let them be for signs and for seasons and for days and years, and let them be lights in the firmament of the heavens to give light upon the earth." And it was so. And God made the two great lights, the greater light to rule the day, and the lesser light to rule the night. . . . And God saw that it was good. (Genesis 1:1, 14-16, 18)

God, who is immaterial and purely spiritual, created matter out of nothing. God, who is changeless and eternal, created time to be the medium for changes in all the material world. He created time, like matter, to observe a certain order. He made the lights in the sky to serve as "signs" for days, seasons, and years. So they have been, in every age, the visible basis for our calendars, which tally our earthly days as lunar months and solar years.

Yet not all of our temporal markers are observable in nature. According to the book of Genesis, God gave the world not only days, months, seasons, and years; he established another marker not based on any natural phenomena—no lights in the sky, or orbits or revolutions—but one simply based on his own example.

> And on the seventh day God finished his work which he had done, and he rested on the seventh day from all his

work which he had done. So God blessed the seventh day and hallowed it, because on it God rested from all his work which he had done in creation. (Genesis 2:1-3)

By completing his labor in six days and resting on the seventh, God instituted the *week*—a temporal unit that is not marked by any signs in the skies or on the earth. Moreover he established its seventh and final day as a "hallowed" day, a holiday set aside for spiritual renewal. Thus the seventh day, the Sabbath, became the original religious festival, the prototype of all the feasts. God ordains this measure of time in the opening pages of the Holy Bible, in the verses that set the stage for all the drama that follows in human history.

From the beginning, then, biblical religion is bound up with concern for the calendar. From the beginning, the religious feasts have given meaning to the days spent in labor.

It is no wonder, then, and it is no accident that seven days without worship should make one weak.

ॐ

The weeks we pass today have their origin in God's commandment. Our rhythm of labor and leisure was established long ago by ritual worship. To us it seems only natural that we should get a "day off" from work. It seems that everyone in the world itself needs to rest at least one day out of seven. That may indeed be true; but if it is, then we know it not from the sun or moon, not from anything in creation, but from the example of the Creator and the traditions of our faith.

The feasts of the Catholic faith are certainly among the most important monuments our ancestors have passed down to us. It

The moon is a primordial religious calendar for Jews and for Christians.

can be argued that the feasts are the primary means by which Christians have handed on the faith.

Today we can publish catechisms by the hundreds of thousands, and we can print Bibles so small that they can fit in a purse or a jacket pocket—or a cell phone. We can do this so economically that almost everyone can afford to own the books. There are even online versions of the Bible and the *Catechism of the Catholic Church* that can be accessed for free.

But for most of Christian history this was not technologically possible. The printing press is a relatively new invention, invented by Johannes Gutenberg around 1439. Before then, the only way to duplicate a book was to copy it out by hand—a very expensive and labor-intensive process. Few people had occasion to read, few had the chance to learn to read, and hardly anyone could afford to own books.

Nevertheless, for close to fifteen hundred years the Church raised up devout generations of worshipers, millions of people who had a lively faith in Jesus Christ and a deep familiarity with his saving doctrine. How was that possible? One of the great Church historians of the last century, Father Josef Jungmann, gave credit to the feasts. The liturgy, he said, "dominated the seasons of the year through the celebration of the ecclesiastical feasts and impressed the chief mysteries of faith upon the popular consciousness."[1] By celebrating Christmas, believers grew in their understanding of the incarnation of the Lord. By observing Good Friday, they came to know the price paid for their redemption. Through the many memorials of the saints and martyrs, ordinary people became familiar with the great historic exemplars of heroic virtue. On Easter—and indeed on every Sunday—they celebrated the glory of God in a human being who is fully alive, who is in fact the fullness of life: Jesus Christ.

Each of the feasts conveyed a truth (or many truths) of the faith. Whether consciously or not, the Christians who established the feasts did so in imitation of God himself. God wants to feed us and fill us, so he gives us banquets at which we can feast spiritually.

The feasts have a lot to teach us. God established them for this reason. Throughout the narrative of the Old Testament, God repeatedly comes to the rescue of his people. It was not

---

1 Josef A. Jungmann, SJ, *Handing on the Faith: A Manual of Catechetics* (New York: Herder and Herder, 1962), 17.

enough that he worked miracles for them. He also insisted that they *remember* the marvels he had done. He required that the remembrance should take the form of a celebration observed on a designated holy day.

> *O give thanks to the Lord,*
> *call on his name,*
> *make known his deeds among the peoples!*
> *Sing to him, sing praises to him,*
> *tell of all his wonderful works!*
> *Glory in his holy name;*
> *let the hearts of those who seek the Lord rejoice!*
>
> . . . .
>
> *Remember the wonderful works that he has done.*
> Psalm 105:1-3, 5

Remembrance is an important dimension of any feast. On Passover, God delivered Israel from slavery in Egypt and saved their firstborn sons from certain death. For that generation, the Passover was surely an unforgettable night; but its memory would have faded with time, and its emotional power would have drained away if God had not commanded that Passover be celebrated as an annual festival: "This day shall be for you a memorial day, and you shall keep it as a feast to the Lord; throughout your generations shall observe it as an ordinance for ever" (Exodus 12:14).

The leisure time and the special foods helped to sweeten the day and make it memorable. But the liturgy made it a *living* memory. For the people of Israel celebrated the Passover not as a past event, but as a reality of the present time. In saving their ancestors, God had saved all subsequent generations. During the ritual meal of the Passover seder, the story of the Exodus is told in the present tense. According to the ancient rabbis, "In every generation a man must so regard himself as if he came forth himself out of Egypt."[2]

The feasts give a sense of common identity to a people scattered all over the world and all through time. Implicit in every celebration is a shared doctrine of God. Every feast celebrates him as all-powerful, as Creator, as King, as Lawgiver, as Redeemer, and as Sanctifier.

For Jews and for Christians, the calendar is a catechism—and it delivers its lessons in a most memorable way. The best-selling Rabbi Harold Kushner explained: "Jews absorbed the central ideas of their faith not by studying them systematically but by celebrating the weekly Sabbath and the annual cycle of festivals, and gradually absorbing the lessons they conveyed."[3]

That is precisely the point Father Jungmann made about Christians through most of history. They *learned* the mysteries of Christianity by *celebrating* the mysteries of Christianity.

It is no less true in an age of widespread literacy. The *Catechism of the Catholic Church* tells us: "The *memorial* is not merely the recollection of past events. . . . In the liturgical celebration of these events, they become in a certain way present and real."[4]

That is how feasts work in biblical religion. They teach, but they don't merely instruct. God does not summon his people

---

2 Mishnah Pesahim 10.5e.

3 Rabbi Harold Kushner, foreword to Hayyim Schauss, *The Jewish Festivals: A Guide to Their History and Observance* (New York: Schocken, 1996), ix.

4 *Catechism of the Catholic Church,* 2nd ed. (Washington, D.C.: USCCB, 1997), 1363; the abbreviation "CCC" is used for citing all subsequent instances in the text.

to attend a history class. A feast teaches by sharing life. The people of today come to participate in a long-ago, saving event. Because the Holy Sacrifice of the Mass is at the center of every Catholic feast, each feast is an occasion of sharing in the life of God. In the celebration of the feasts, God's salvation is not simply past, but really present.

The feasts are a way of remembering the past, and we celebrate them in the present. But they encompass still another dimension. They anticipate a final fulfillment in the future. In the Old Testament, the prophet Isaiah foretold a day when the Lord would bring peace and unity to all the peoples of the world. He imagined that day as a banquet, a feast.

On this mountain the Lord of hosts will make for all peoples a feast of fat things, a feast of wine on the lees, of fat things full of marrow, of wine on the lees well refined. And he will destroy on this mountain the covering that is cast over all peoples, the veil that is spread over all nations. He will swallow up death for ever, and the Lord GOD will wipe away tears from all faces, and the reproach of his people he will take away from all the earth; for the Lord has spoken. It will be said on that day, "Lo, this is our God; we have waited for him, that he might save us. This is the Lord; we have waited for him; let us be glad and rejoice in his salvation." (Isaiah 25:6-9)

The biblical feasts are times of great joy, yet they are only a sample, a foretaste of the true feast to come. Through the oracles of the prophet, the Lord revealed that his anointed—the *Messiah,* the *Christ*—would establish the kingdom of God, and that kingdom would be characterized as a perpetual feast.

The New Testament shows Jesus's life to be a fulfillment of that prophecy. Saint Luke arranges his narrative of Jesus's ministry around a succession of ten banquets, beginning with the dinner hosted by Levi the tax collector and ending with the postresurrection supper at Emmaus. The Gospel's pre-eminent feast, of course, is the Last Supper, at which Jesus established the Eucharist as his memorial, to be observed till the end of time.

With the Eucharist, fulfillment arrived. The letter to the Hebrews describes the Church's liturgy in terms that evoke Isaiah's feast upon the mountain: "you have come to Mount Zion and to the city of the living God, the heavenly Jerusalem, and to innumerable angels in festal gathering" (Hebrews 12:22). At the Church's Eucharist, the angels of heaven gather with the faithful on earth to celebrate the Lord's great feast.

Yet even this greatest of feasts anticipates a plenary fulfillment. The book of Revelation shows the culmination of all history as "the marriage supper of the Lamb" (Revelation 19:9). The description clearly refers to the Eucharist, when God comes to dwell with his people, but also to a time when God "will wipe away every tear from their eyes, and death shall be no more, neither shall there be mourning nor crying nor pain any more, for the former things have passed away" (Revelation 21:4).

Before he was elected pope, Cardinal Joseph Ratzinger spoke of the Christian feast as "the 'already' entering our 'not yet,'"[5] and he compared it to Jesus's miracle at the wedding banquet of Cana (see John 2). Jesus's hour had not yet come, yet he fulfilled the prayer of his mother and changed ordinary water to wine for the celebration.

Our earthly feasts are a joyful anticipation of greater days still ahead: the definitive Day of the Lord. When we feast on earth, we show our confidence in the promises of heaven.

❧

Past, present, and future converge when we celebrate the feasts. We truly participate in events of long ago, and we anticipate the glories of the future. Yet we never leave the present moment.

This is what happens when eternity comes rushing into time, as it did when the Word became flesh and made his dwell-

---

5 Joseph Cardinal Ratzinger, *A New Song for the Lord: Faith in Christ and Liturgy Today* (New York: Crossroad, 1996), 129.

ing among us (John 1:14). This is what the feasts make possible. Past, present, and future unite in a single moment. It's more mind-boggling than any thought experiment you read about in high-school physics. Yet it's more plausible than any time travel scheme you've seen in science fiction movies.

The eternal feast is fulfilled now, in our feasts and through the liturgy, and it is never-ending. Yet we continue to mark it off by increments of time, until the close of the age. It is present as the mystery at the heart of all the feasts of the Church.

At the feasts we grow strong in Christ. God created us for such celebration, and we should never wait long for it, not even seven days.

CHAPTER 2

Reasons to Feast

For it is a jubilee; it shall be holy to you;
you shall eat what it yields out of the field.
—Leviticus 25:12

THE PRIMAL WEEK ENDS with a feast day, the Sabbath. All the world was created for that end: to glorify God in festive worship. This is fundamental Catholic doctrine. The *Catechism of the Catholic Church* tells us:

> Creation was fashioned with a view to the sabbath and therefore for the worship and adoration of God. Worship is inscribed in the order of creation (cf. Gen 1:14). As the rule of St. Benedict says, nothing should take precedence over "the work of God," that is, solemn worship (St. Benedict, *Regula* 43,3: PL 66,675–676). This indicates the right order of human concerns. (CCC 347)

Adam and Eve, man and woman, were created for the sake of celebration. Their lives would have been weak and incomplete without it.

This does not mean that paradise was an endless birthday party. The Genesis account makes it clear that God created us to work for a living. When he made the first man and woman out of dust, he commanded them to "fill the earth and subdue it; and have dominion over . . . every living thing that moves upon the earth" (Genesis 1:28). "The Lord God took the man and put him in the garden of Eden to till it and keep it" (Genesis 2:15).

We were "put" on earth to work the earth. We're hardwired for labor, and we won't be satisfied unless we fulfill God's command.

Yet that's not the end of the story. For work is ordered to something greater. God's six days of "labor," his six days of creation, are ordered to a Sabbath of rest. "And on the seventh day God finished his work which he had done, and he rested on the seventh day from all his work which he had done" (Genesis 2:2).

Historical critics arch an eyebrow at the line and dismiss it as anthropomorphism—the tendency that primitive peoples had to project human qualities onto God. But the Church Fathers and early rabbis had a clearer sense of the sacred text and its sacred meaning.

Our work is service due to God. He commanded it, and it is necessary (by his design) for the continuing creation and sanctification of the world. Nevertheless, our more important service is *worship,* and the prerequisite of worship is leisure: the seventh day. As one rabbi put it, the Sabbath is "last in creation, first in intention."

If God is who we say he is—almighty and unchanging—he doesn't grow tired, and he never needs to rest. If he did "take a rest" in the Genesis narrative, he did so, like a good father, in order to show his children how to do it. He was modeling the leisure he wanted us to keep, and he institutionalized it in the Sabbath.

It's almost as if God was daring us to trust him—to let go of the plow (or the computer keyboard, or the tool chest) and rest in confidence that the Creator who started the job can finish it just fine, with or without our eight- or ten-hour days. When we celebrate our feast days, we are showing God that we trust him. It's an outward sign of our innermost faith, a visible sign of a spiritual reality. Feast days, in that sense, are deeply sacramental.

There are, of course, benefits to our feast days in the natural order. Our bodies need rest. Our minds need rest. Aristotle was a practical man, and he saw the benefits of leisure. In his

Nicomachean Ethics Aristotle wrote: "Since we cannot work forever, we need relaxation." Rest, he said, is "a means to activity" (10.6). Modern research has confirmed that employees who rest are indeed more productive than employees who work without ceasing.

As believers, we do not deny such benefits in the natural order; but, again, we recognize that there is something more to the story.

In his profound little book called *The Sabbath,* Rabbi Abraham Joshua Heschel observes that Aristotle got things exactly backward. "To the biblical mind . . . labor is the means toward an end, and the Sabbath as a day of rest, as a day of abstaining from toil, is not for the purpose of recovering one's lost strength and becoming fit for the forthcoming labor. The Sabbath is a day for the sake of life. . . . The Sabbath is not for the sake of the weekdays; the weekdays are for the sake of Sabbath. *It is not an interlude but the climax of living.*"[1]

Since the Sabbath is the prototype of all the feasts of both Christians and Jews, that is the truth at the bottom of every celebration.

᷒ᓎ

When we celebrate the feast days, we are living life to the full, because we are fulfilling a deep need in human nature. God made us fundamentally to desire joy. And we want to have a reason for joy.

At the time Christianity appeared, the Roman world ob-

---

1 Abraham Joshua Heschel, *The Sabbath: Its Meaning for Modern Man* (New York: Farrar, Straus and Giroux, 1990), 14; emphasis added.

served a calendar with ample time for partying. There was no shortage of civil and religious holidays. In fact, it was the excess of holidays that moved Julius Caesar to reform the calendar. There were many feasts, and their banquets were marked by "reveling and drunkenness . . . debauchery and licentiousness" (Romans 13:13). They were unfettered affairs with unlimited physical pleasures, yet these occasions were unsatisfying and joyless, ending often enough in "quarreling and jealousy" (ibid).

The Christian feasts are a different matter altogether. They celebrate something that truly inspires joy—and even requires joy. The key, once again, is in the creation story. On the Sabbath day, God's people take the fruits of their labors—the production of the other six days—and offer them all to God as worship.

Thus, Christians have always celebrated the feasts with the best that creation has to offer: meats and sweets, fruits, wine, flowers, music, dancing, art, poetry. The celebration is all in good order, all in good measure, because it is ordered to an ultimate end: to God.

Raised up to God, the things of creation become a monument to divine generosity and Providence—God's fatherly love and spousal tenderness toward his people.

The Catholic philosopher Josef Pieper spent a long lifetime pondering the meaning of our feasting. He worked out a profound "theory of festivity" in a book he titled *In Tune with the World*. He observed, "A festival is essentially a phenomenon of wealth; not, to be sure, the wealth of money, but of existential richness."[2] Every time we celebrate a feast it is as if we are drawing upon a family inheritance again and again, yet it never diminishes. In fact, a Christian life grows richer with every passing holy day. A very old man carries within him the memories of Christmases in his earliest childhood. If he loses his home and all his savings, those memories will continue to bring him profound joy, which is what God made him to desire. What's more, because he is Christian, he will always have a reason to celebrate the feasts again. "Jesus Christ is the same yesterday and today and for ever" (Hebrews 13:8).

With every feast, God's people celebrate the Creator by means of the goodness of creation. To celebrate is to affirm that the world is good. God made it so and declared it so (Genesis 1:31); and he loved the world so much that he sent his only Son to save it (John 3:16). These facts alone are sufficient reason to fill a calendar with celebrations. "To celebrate a festival means,"

---

2 Josef Pieper, *In Tune with the World: A Theory of Festivity* (South Bend, Ind.: St. Augustine's Press, 1999), 19.

according to Pieper, "to live out, for some special occasion and in an uncommon manner, the universal assent to the world as a whole."[3]

In the feasts we recognize that God has given us a good life, and we "have it abundantly" (John 10:10). The feasts are a fixed occasion to indulge in the joy God made us to desire—and made us to possess in the end.

Without the feasts of our faith, life would be incomplete. Apart from God, all the partying in the world would leave its revelers unsatisfied and restless. Festivity turns joyless when it lacks a transcendent focus. It's not enough merely to spread the table and pour the wine. There must be a reason for the celebration; and the reason must be inexhaustible in order to fill feast after feast in century after century.

PIEPER RECOGNIZED THAT TRUE joy arises from love: "the reason for joy . . . is always the same: possessing or receiving what one loves, whether actually in the present, hoped for in the future, or remembered in the past."[4] That's why we throw parties when couples get engaged, or get married, or mark significant wedding anniversaries.

The feasts of Christ are like these family joys, only on a grand scale. They are universal. They are eternal. They provide true joy that satisfies.

We can enjoy the world, even with its sufferings, and we can celebrate life, with all its ups and downs, when we see the world, our lives, and our salvation as gifts from God who loves us. *That* is the only true cause for celebration.

---

3 Ibid., 30.
4 Ibid., 22–23.

CHAPTER 3

The Feasts That Jesus Kept

So teach us to number our days
that we may get a heart of wisdom.
—Psalm 90:12

JESUS WAS FORMED BY THE FEASTS. A devout Jew, he was raised in a home with parents who dutifully observed the calendar. He learned to number his days a certain way—most significantly by sevens. His family might have fasted twice a week, on Monday and Thursday. We know that it was "his custom" to go to the synagogue for worship every Sabbath (see Luke 4:15). It was his family's custom to go "to Jerusalem every year at the feast of the Passover" (Luke 2:41-42).

Luke's Gospel tells us that, through his childhood and youth, "Jesus increased in wisdom and in stature" (Luke 2:52). That is true for Jesus just as it is for any boy or girl. Yet the only evidence the evangelists bring forth to explain his progress is related to the religious feasts. Jesus developed not only because the years passed, but also because his family engaged in prayer in accordance with the calendar and the established customs.

The Child Jesus in the Temple.

God had instituted the Sabbath at the creation of the world and had decreed in one of the Ten Commandments that the seventh day be set aside as a day of rest: "Remember the Sabbath day, to keep it holy" (see Exodus 20:8-11). It was also God's Law, given through Moses, that required all adult males in Israel to celebrate three pilgrim feasts every year in the holy city, Jerusalem (Exodus 23:14). God summoned his people together to celebrate Passover (Pesach), the Feast of Weeks (Shavuot, sometimes translated as Pentecost), and the Feast of Tents (Sukkot, sometimes translated as Tabernacles or Booths).

In addition to these three feasts, the Jews of Jesus's time celebrated four other major feasts: New Year (Rosh Hashanah); the Day of Atonement (Yom Kippur); the Feast of Dedication or Feast of Lights (Hanukkah); and the Feast of Lots (Purim). There were other feasts as well. One of Jesus's contemporaries, a Jewish philosopher named Philo of Alexandria, spoke of ten significant festivals, including the seven we have already mentioned, plus the Sabbath and the new moon that began each month.

The first festival, according to Philo, is one that "anyone will perhaps be astonished to hear called a festival. This festival is every day."

Philo taught that any Jew who was perfectly faithful to the law should experience all of life as a festival. Such people, he said, are "very naturally rendered cheerful by their virtues" and "pass the whole of their lives as a festival."[1]

Most people are not so virtuous; they often feel oppressed by the evils in the world and by their own uneasy conscience. In fact, Philo acknowledged that, strictly speaking, "the feasts

---

1 Philo, *Special Laws* 2.41–46.

belong to God alone; for he alone is happy and blessed, having no participation in any evil whatsoever."[2]

God, then, did not need special feasts. Nor does he need them today. Yet he commanded them. God made their celebration obligatory and laid it down as law.

It seems odd that God should have to enact a law requiring people to enjoy a day of leisure and joyful worship. But it was as true in the days of Philo and Jesus as it is today: many people will not relax unless they are required to do so. They live workaholic weeks with no time to spare for God. Even worse, they pressure others to live that way. Employees, coworkers, and vendors find that they are expected to be on the job when they really should be at worship. And oftentimes parents find themselves having to bring their children to sports practices or events when they should be at church.

God made holy days *obligatory* to protect all his people; he exerts his own divine pressure for the good of both the powerful and the vulnerable. The vulnerable need the shelter and consolation of the feasts, so they need to be protected from their overlords, who could deny them the freedom to celebrate. But the powerful, too, need the feasts; and God made the Law to protect them from themselves.

Israel's labor laws were humane because their feasts were obligatory, and their feasts kept the nation's focus on God—every week, every month, all year, and three times a year in Jerusalem.

2 Ibid., 2.11.53.

Long after he left his childhood home, Jesus continued to observe the feasts. We have already seen in Saint Luke's Gospel that Jesus celebrated the Sabbath and the Passover. Saint John shows Jesus celebrating these as well as the Feast of Booths (John 7:2), the Feast of Dedication (John 10:22), and possibly the Feast of Weeks (John 5:1).

Since Jesus is God, we must assume that his faithful celebration of the Sabbath and the feasts was not for his own benefit. If anyone could live the perpetual feast described by Philo, Jesus could. He is true God and true man. He is sinless and impeccable.

Why, then, did he celebrate the feasts? Because he was the pioneer of our salvation (see Hebrews 2:10 and 12:2). He lived in a way that would be salutary for all of us who follow after him. We imitate him. We share his life. And so we observe the feasts of God, as he did.

Yet we observe our feasts in a different way. From a Christian perspective, all the feasts of the Old Testament found their fulfillment in Jesus Christ. He appears as the Passover Lamb foreshadowed in every celebration since the Exodus (see John 1:29). He appears as the New Temple, dedicated not by King Solomon or Zerubbabel or Herod, but by God (see John 2:21 and 10:22). He appears as the source of abundant spiritual refreshment in the world, fulfilling the rites of the "Great Day" of the Feast of Tabernacles (see John 7:37).

The feasts of the Old Testament were "memorials." The Hebrew term was *zikkaron,* along with its close cousin *azkarah,* and it denotes a particular kind of sacrifice: "and the priest shall burn this as its *memorial* portion upon the altar, an offering by fire, a pleasing odor to the Lord" (Leviticus 2:2). The Greek

Jews translated *zikkaron* with the word *anamnesis,* from which root we English-speakers have drawn our words *memory, memorial,* and *remembrance.*

It was at a Passover meal that Jesus instituted the new feast that would draw together the family of God, and he spoke of the event in terms of remembrance.

> And he took bread, and when he had given thanks he broke it and gave it to them, saying, "This is my body which is given for you. Do this in remembrance of me." And likewise the cup after supper, saying, "This cup which is poured out for you is the new covenant in my blood." (Luke 22:19-20)

Jesus established his new feast of victory, his new Passover, in terms that were explicitly sacrificial and priestly. He gave the Eucharist to be his memorial sacrifice.

The Church has always celebrated the Mass in these terms. Christians have most commonly associated the Mass with the Passover, the "paschal mystery" of Jesus's suffering, death, and resurrection.

Saint Paul, in the New Testament's earliest reference to the Eucharist, says: "Christ, our paschal lamb, has been sacrificed. Let us, therefore, celebrate the festival, not with the old leaven, the leaven of malice and evil, but with the unleavened bread of sincerity and truth" (1 Corinthians 5:7-8).

Christ is the new festival, the feast of the Church. He is the new Passover Lamb, truly present in the "unleavened bread" of the Eucharist.

The language we use today in the Holy Sacrifice of the Mass is just as redolent of Jesus's seder meal in the Upper Room. In our Eucharistic Prayer, the priest prays to God the Father: "Look with favor on the oblation of your Church, in which we show forth the paschal Sacrifice of Christ that has been handed on to us."[3]

Every Mass is a participation in the once-for-all sacrifice of Jesus Christ. Every Mass shares in Jesus's paschal mystery. The *Catechism* captures the Church's sense of wonder, which we should make our own:

In the liturgy of the Church, it is principally his own Paschal mystery that Christ signifies and makes present. During his earthly life Jesus announced his Paschal mystery by his teaching and anticipated it by his actions. When his Hour comes, he lives out the unique event of history

---

3 *Roman Missal*, "Eucharistic Prayer for Use in Masses for Various Needs."

which does not pass away: Jesus dies, is buried, rises from the dead, and is seated at the right hand of the Father "once for all" (Rom 6:10; Heb 7:27; 9:12; cf. Jn 13:1; 17:1). His Paschal mystery is a real event that occurred in our history, but it is unique: all other historical events happen once, and then they pass away, swallowed up in the past. The Paschal mystery of Christ, by contrast, cannot remain only in the past, because by his death he destroyed death, and all that Christ is—all that he did and suffered for all men—participates in the divine eternity, and so transcends all times while being made present in them all. The event of the Cross and Resurrection *abides* and draws everything toward life. (CCC, 1085)

Saint John Paul II also stressed the importance of the Eucharist in the encyclical *Ecclesia de Eucharistia*:

When the Church celebrates the Eucharist, the memorial of her Lord's death and resurrection, this central event of salvation becomes really present and "the work of our redemption is carried out" (Lumen Gentium 3).[4]

That is why the Eucharist is the banquet at the center of every Christian feast. It is the feast of victory for our God. If we celebrate Jesus's conception, birth, baptism, and transfiguration—if we celebrate his mother's assumption into heaven—and if we celebrate the salvation he worked in and through the lives of Saint Jude Thaddeus, Saint Francis of Assisi, Saint Pio of Pie-

---

4 John Paul II, *Ecclesia de Eucharistia* (On the Eucharist and Its Relationship to the Church), April 17, 2003, 11.

trelcina, and Blessed Mother Teresa of Calcutta, among others, then we celebrate because we view all these events through the lens of his paschal mystery.

The Mass is the way Jesus chose to extend the events of salvation through all time and into every Christian life. Jesus established his memorial sacrifice for us and for our salvation.

ॐ

The early Christians delighted in finding the parallels between the ancient Passover and its fulfillment in Christ. But the Mass is also the Day of Atonement—when the eternal priest enters the heavenly holy of holies, just as the earthly high priest did in the Jerusalem Temple on Yom Kippur (Hebrews 9:24-26). The Mass is the new Pentecost, when the Spirit is given to God's people.

Also from the apostolic generation onward the Mass was ordinarily celebrated on Sunday, the first day of the week, which emerged as the Church's weekly holy day, distinct from the Sabbath of the Old Testament. So central was the Mass to every Lord's Day that the Christians of the third century referred to the Eucharist simply as *Dominica*, "the Sunday."

The American novelist William Faulkner famously said, "The past is never dead. It's not even past." That is true especially of the feasts. Though we do not celebrate the festivals in the same ways that Jesus and his contemporaries did, we celebrate the same works of God, which are now brought to perfection and fulfillment in Jesus.

Jesus said: "Think not that I have come to abolish the law and the prophets; I have come not to abolish them but to fulfil them. For truly, I say to you, till heaven and earth pass away, not an iota, not a dot, will pass from the law until all is accomplished" (Matthew 5:17-18).

As we examine the individual feasts of the contemporary Church—Sunday, Easter, Pentecost, and so on—we will return often to their roots in the history of God's chosen people, Israel. We cannot fully understand our worship today apart from careful study of the piety practiced by Jesus, Mary, and Joseph, and all the apostles and holy women of the New Testament. They were observant Jews, and they kept the feasts. We keep the feasts because we are faithful to the tradition they have passed on to us. In the words of Pope Pius XI, "spiritually we are all Semites."[5]

The feasts of ancient times, the feasts that Jesus knew, are still very much with us as we celebrate the feasts of the Church. They are with us, in fact, in every Mass; and they arrive as still greater cause for celebration.

---

5 Pope Pius XI, address to Belgian pilgrims at the Vatican, September 6, 1938.

CHAPTER 4

A Brief History of Time: On the Development of the Calendar and Its Books

But as to the times and the seasons, brethren,
you have no need to have anything written to you.
—1 Thessalonians 5:1

CHRISTIANS TODAY CAN FIND MUCH that is familiar in the calendar kept by Jews in the time of Jesus Christ. There are, of course, great differences as well. The Church began, in its first generation, to recast the year to convey the mysteries of God and salvation in new terms—terms of fulfillment in Jesus, the Messiah—and the process continued through the subsequent generations. It is still going on today.

The transition was difficult at first, especially for Jewish Christians, and the strain is evident in the New Testament. God's people had experienced history's most important moment—a moment that seemed to transform everything. For the Jews who believed in Jesus, salvation in Christ changed the way they interpreted the past. It changed the way they looked to the future. How should that transformation be reflected in the calendar and its feast days? What should be altered? What should stay the same?

It's clear that there was spirited debate among the early Christians. Saint Paul described the situation in his letter to the Romans: "One man esteems one day as better than another, while another man esteems all days alike" (Romans 14:5). He went on to make a plea for patience and tolerance amid a diversity of opinions: "Let every one be fully convinced in his own mind." Similarly, he told the Colossians: "let no one pass judgment on you in questions of food and drink or with regard to a festival or a new moon or a sabbath" (Colossians 2:16). The Church was working the matter out, and the process would take time.

Paul's life showed the strain of the transformation. In the Acts of the Apostles we find him "hastening to be at Jerusalem, if possible, on the day of Pentecost" (Acts 20:16). He was eager to celebrate the old feast the old way, in the holy city, though presumably with a new focus. Yet he also faulted the Galatians for their scrupulosity over the calendar: "You observe days, and months, and seasons, and years!" (Galatians 4:10).

The Christian calendar did not emerge fully formed with the establishment of the Church. It took centuries for the apostles and their successors to fashion a full year ordered to the paschal mystery.

꧁꧂

From the beginning, Christians observed Sunday as the Lord's Day, a weekly commemoration of Jesus's resurrection (see Acts 20:7, Revelation 1:10). Some, however, also kept the Sabbath in a traditional Jewish way, as a day of rest—and as a day of preparation for the feast on Sunday.

As the day of the weekly feast changed, so did the traditional days of fasting. It was the custom of Jews to fast on Mondays and Thursdays. Christians in the first century fasted on Wednesdays and Fridays, the latter day to recall the crucifixion and death of Jesus. Over time the Church would reduce its universal fast to Fridays alone.

Christians continued to keep the great feasts of Passover and Pentecost, though the observance varied over time and according to the various churches. In the churches of the Eastern lands, the custom was to celebrate Easter on the same day as the Jewish Passover, the fifteenth day of the month Nisan on the Hebrew calendar. The Western churches always observed the feast on a Sunday near Passover. Christians found this difference unbearable, as it touched upon their most important feast. The Church, everyone agreed, should celebrate the feast together. Unfortunately, Christians did not always air their differences in the most charitable ways, and the dispute over the celebration of Easter threatened many times to divide the Church into warring factions. The matter was not settled until the world's bishops, at the Council of Nicaea in AD 325, made the decision to celebrate Easter always on a Sunday—the first Sunday following the first full moon after the spring equinox, to be precise.

Other feasts arose in those first centuries. Some local churches celebrated the Lord's baptism with a special day. Some observed the annunciation of his birth with special days. The dates varied at first, as we'll see in later chapters.

From very early times the churches also kept memorials of their local heroes—the Christians who had died as martyrs.

Outside the New Testament, the oldest account of a particular martyr's death is *The Martyrdom of Polycarp,* which was set down in the mid-100s. It concludes with a rather precise date stamp: "Now, the blessed Polycarp suffered martyrdom on the second day of the month Xanthicus just begun, the seventh day before the Kalends of May, on the great Sabbath, at the eighth hour."[1] The author did this for the benefit of the Church of Smyrna, which observed the feast of its martyr-bishop on that date every year.

This custom was not peculiar to Smyrna. Churches everywhere did the same. They observed each martyr's passing as a *dies natalis,* a birthday: the day they were born into heaven, the next and definitive state of Christian life. From Carthage, North Africa, we have dates for the deaths of Saints Perpetua and Felicity (AD March 7, 203), Saint Cyprian (September 14, 258), and many other martyrs. From Alexandria, Egypt, we have the dates of hundreds more. Gradually, in the course of the first five hundred years after the life of Christ, the Church in Rome began to collect these dates into a large "martyrology"—a calendar for the universal Church setting down the days of celebration for the great saints from all over the world. From the fourth century onward, non-martyr saints also begin to appear on the various Christian calendars.

The Church also continued to deepen its reflection on the mysteries of Christ and over time added feasts to commemorate many major and minor aspects of his earthly life: from his circumcision to the transfiguration on Mount Tabor, from the epiphany to his Kingship, from the exaltation of his cross to his abiding presence in the Eucharist.

---

1 *Martyrdom of Polycarp,* 21.

By the end of the Middle Ages, the calendar was thick with celebrations—and maybe *too* thick. Theologians and bishops worried that the proliferation of saints' feasts had produced a misshapen Church year. With so many required celebrations, it was hard to keep a congregation's focus on the season, or indeed on the centrality of the paschal mystery. The Council of Trent (1545–1563) called for an overhaul of the calendar, and Pope Saint Pius V produced a new calendar soon afterward.

More work was needed, however, and the Church took up the task again in the twentieth century. In 1911 Pope Saint Pius X streamlined the order of psalms and prayers that were recited in the Divine Office by priests and members of religious orders. Pope Pius XII, whose pontificate lasted from 1939 to 1958, instituted reforms that significantly changed the way Catholics experienced the great days of the calendar, especially the days of Holy Week and the Easter Triduum. He wanted *not* to introduce innovations, but rather to return to the original spirit of the celebrations, as we find them in the most ancient sources, in the writings of the New Testament and the early Church Fathers. The Second Vatican Council (1962–1965) recognized the need for still more work on the calendar. It was left to Venerable Pope Paul VI to produce the monumental work of reform with his 1969 document *Mysterii Paschalis (*on the Liturgical Year and the New Universal Roman Calendar). He began the document with a statement of his concerns in undertaking such a sweeping reform.

The Paschal Mystery and its celebration constitutes the essence of Christian worship in its daily, weekly and yearly unfolding. The Second Vatican Council clearly teaches this. It follows therefore that the restoration of the liturgical

year, whose norms have been formulated by the same Holy
Synod, must put this Paschal Mystery in sharper focus with
regard to the organization of the Proper of the Season and
the Proper of the Saints as well as in the revision of the
Roman Calendar.

It is true that in the course of time the multiplication of
feasts, vigils and octaves, as well as the progressive compli-
cation of different parts of the liturgical year, have often
driven the faithful to particular devotions, in such a way
that their minds have been somewhat diverted from the
fundamental mysteries of our Redemption.[2]

"Sharper focus"—those words serve as an excellent summary of the work of Paul VI, but also of his predecessors, especially Pius V, Pius X, and Pius XII. They wanted to simplify
the calendar in order to improve the quality of worship. They
wanted people to walk attentively in the footsteps of Christ
through all the seasons of the year, without detours.

The trend over recent centuries has been to emphasize the
major feasts—Christmas, Easter, and Pentecost—and to restore
Sunday to its preeminence as the "original feast day."[3] This
required the pruning of some saints' days; but other, modern
saints were added to the Church's calendar.

That wasn't the end of the story, though. Pope Saint John
Paul II added a few new celebrations during his papal ministry
(1978–2005) and restored some older ones.

The truth is that there will be no "end of the story" for the

---

2 Pope Paul VI, *Mysterii Paschalis (motu proprio,* on the Liturgical Year and the New Universal Roman Calendar), *February 14, 1969,* 1.

3 Second Vatican Council, *Sacrosanctum Concilium (*Constitution on the Sacred Liturgy),
December 4, 1963, 106.

calendar until the end of time! The Church's calendar will always be a work in progress. The popes will always be adjusting our seasons and celebrations, because the Church will always be deepening its reflection on the mysteries of the Lord—and manifesting God's holiness in the lives of new saints. All of that reflection, and all of that holiness, must inevitably affect the shape of the calendar.

☙❧

With the reform of the calendar came a reform in the Church's liturgical books. The lectionary—which prescribes the Scripture readings for every Mass—received a thoroughgoing revision in the 1960s. In fact, the Church changed the basic structure of the lectionary.

For centuries the Church's lectionary had followed a one-year cycle of Sunday readings. With the lectionary published in 1969, the cycle expanded to *three* years, so that more of the Bible could be included in the public readings of the Church. Year A generally follows the Gospel of Matthew; Year B follows Mark; and Year C follows Luke. John's Gospel appears in all three years, especially during the important seasons and feasts.

For centuries the weekday readings had also followed a one-year cycle. Now they follow a two-year cycle.

There used to be two Sunday readings: the first from one of the New Testament letters, the second from one of the Gospels. But since 1969 there have been three Sunday readings: the first is usually from the Old Testament; the second from the New Testament letters; and the third from one of the Gospels. Again, in this way a lot more of the Bible is read publicly at Mass.

The books of the Bible were originally composed and

compiled for the sake of public recitation. Remember, in the ancient world private study was a rare luxury. Even before the rise of Christianity, the Jews in exile divided the books of the Law and the Prophets so that they could be read in synagogues over the course of a year or two years of Sabbaths. In the first century, Saint Paul observed: "For from early generations Moses has had in every city those who preach him, for he is read every sabbath in the synagogues" (Acts 15:21). The ancient rabbis traced the custom of using appointed readings for worship all the way back to Moses himself.

The early Christians likely adapted the synagogue lectionary as they developed their own liturgy. Around the year 150, Saint Justin Martyr described a typical Mass in the city of Rome, noting that "the memoirs of the Apostles and the writings of the prophets are read."[4]

The sermons of the later Church Fathers seem to suggest that preachers in far-flung lands were using similar texts on the Church's feasts. Scholars have recovered or reconstructed lectionaries from the ancient churches in the lands that are now Italy, Spain, France, Syria, Armenia, Tunisia, and Georgia.

The ancient lectionaries, like their modern counterparts, show us that Christians kept their feasts with careful observance, an abundance of Scripture, and—always—the singing of Psalms.

The lectionaries show, too, how worship unites Christians, even when they are geographically distant and unable to communicate with ease. Simply by keeping the Church's calendar and following its liturgical books, Christians can make sure they are all on the same page.

---

4 Saint Justin Martyr, *First Apology,* 67.

CHAPTER 5

Terms of the Times

Why is any day better than another,
when all the daylight in the year is from the sun?
By the Lord's decision they were distinguished,
and he appointed the different seasons and feasts;
some of them he exalted and hallowed,
and some of them he made ordinary days.
—Sirach 33:7-9

AS WE SAW IN THE story of creation, not all days are created equal. Some are more important, liturgically speaking, than others. Some days mark greater joys and thus require more from the Christians who celebrate them.

The Church classifies its days according to five basic categories: Sunday, Solemnity, Feast, Memorial, and Seasonal Weekday. The day's ranking will determine which prayers are said at Mass. Relative rank will also determine which observance takes priority when, say, a "memorial" falls on the same day as a "solemnity"—or if either falls on a Sunday. Only solemnities (and a few select feasts) may take priority over a Sunday.

In this book so far we have used the term "feasts" in its colloquial sense, to denote all special days in the Church's calendar. The word also has a technical sense when it is used to describe a certain rank of observance. We will continue to use the word in both senses; the meaning should always be clear from context.

Sunday—The Lord's Day is the great day of the Christian calendar. It is the day each week when the whole Church gathers to celebrate salvation in Jesus Christ by attending his festal banquet, the Mass. The regularly scheduled Sunday celebration outranks most other days that might coincide with it. The exceptions to this rule are the solemnities, a few of the feasts, and just one of the memorials (All Souls).

Solemnity—This is the most important Christian celebration—the first rank of liturgical days. A solemnity commemorates one of the principal mysteries of the faith—important events in the life of Our Lord, Our Lady, or the Church. Christmas, the Assumption, and Pentecost, for example, are solemnities. Jesus's Kingship is celebrated with a solemnity (Christ the King) as is his Sacred Heart. A few solemnities are dedicated to saints of universal importance, such as Saint Joseph as well as Saints Peter and Paul. The Mass of a solemnity is like a Sunday Mass. It has three prescribed readings from Scripture; it has its own proper prayers; and the congregation recites the Gloria and the Creed. When a solemnity falls on a Sunday, it is celebrated instead of Sunday. (If a solemnity falls on a Sunday in Advent or Lent, however, or during Holy Week or the Easter Octave, it will be transferred to the following Monday.)

Feast—Feasts are similar to solemnities in the range of celebrations they cover. The feasts honor certain mysteries of the lives of Jesus and Mary as well as some of their titles. They also pay homage to an elite group of saints, such as the apostles, who are important to the whole Church. Some feasts commemorate important events in Church history, such as the dedication of the ancient Roman basilicas. All of the mysteries and saints we celebrate in the feasts are *important,* but not as *central* to the faith as those we mark with solemnities. The feasts commemorate events or persons of a lesser theological significance than those marked by the solemnities. We commemorate Jesus's baptism with a feast, for example, but his resurrection with a solemnity. We mark Mary's visitation with a feast, but the Lord's annunciation with a solemnity. The Mass for a feast will differ from a Sunday Mass in some ways. It will have its own proper prayers, but there are only two Scripture readings. It will include the Gloria but not the Creed. When the feasts that honor Jesus (such as the Exaltation of the Cross) fall on a weekday, they are celebrated with all the elements that make up a Sunday Mass.

Memorial—Most memorials are dedicated to particular saints, though some belong to the lesser mysteries of Our Lord or Our Lady. The Holy Name of Jesus and the Holy Name of Mary, for instance, are marked by memorials (January 3 and September 12, respectively). Some memorials are always observed, while others are optional. If a memorial is obligatory, then the Mass of the day will include prescribed prayers that are appropriate to the occasion and sometimes special Scripture readings as well. The memorials of historically important saints—such as Francis of Assisi and Ignatius of Loyola—are obligatory for the universal Church. Some optional memorials have special prayers and readings, but they are not used unless the priest-celebrant chooses to observe the day.

Weekday (in Latin, *feria*)—This is the term for a day other than Sunday in any of the five major liturgical seasons: Advent, Christmas, Lent, Easter, and Ordinary Time. Unless the day is a solemnity, feast, or memorial, it is observed simply as, for example, "Wednesday of the Third Week of Lent," "Tuesday of the Eighteenth Week in Ordinary Time," and so on.

The classification of some liturgical days varies from country to country. Local churches tend to honor their local saints and favorite devotions in a special way. The Church in Ireland keeps Saint Patrick's Day as a solemnity, though it is only a memorial on the universal calendar. Similarly, the feast of Saint Andrew is a solemnity in Scotland. Catholics in Argentina honor the country's patroness, Our Lady of Luján, with a solemnity on May 8.

☙

How are the dates of the feasts determined? Many are traditional, having been passed down from the earliest generations of the Church. The feasts and memorials of saints are usually set on the anniversary of their death. The celebration may fall on another date that the Church judges to be more appropriate. The feast of Saint Ambrose of Milan, for example, is observed on the date of his consecration as bishop.

Some feasts are matched to a day that is apt or fitting because of its temporal season or because of a coincidental secular occasion. The Memorial of Saint Joseph the Worker was set on May 1 because the labor movement had kept the date as International Workers Day since the 1800s.

Some feasts are fixed, while others are moveable. Fixed feasts occur on the same date every year; Christmas is fixed, always on December 25. Easter is moveable, as are the feasts whose position every year depends on when Easter occurs (including the Ascension, Pentecost, the Most Holy Trinity, Corpus Christi, the Sacred Heart of Jesus, and the Immaculate Heart of Mary).

☙❧

Certain feasts are so important to Christian life that they must not be forgotten or neglected. God commanded his people to "*Remember* the Sabbath and keep it holy." Thus Catholic believers are required to attend Mass on Sunday, to keep the remembrance in the way Jesus commanded.

Some solemnities, too, are so important that they are observed as if they were Sundays; thus their observance is obligatory for all Catholics. We call them *holy days of obligation*. They are the holidays, besides Sunday, when Catholics are expected to attend Mass. On those days we are also asked "to abstain from those works and affairs which hinder the worship to be

The Church's solemnities are especially festive celebrations.

rendered to God, the joy proper to the Lord's day, or the suitable relaxation of mind and body."[1]

In the universal Church, there are ten holy days of obligation:

Mary, Mother of God (January 1)
Epiphany (January 6)
Saint Joseph (March 19)
Ascension (forty days after Easter)
Corpus Christi (also known as the Most Holy Body and
　　Blood of Christ, Thursday after Trinity Sunday)
Saints Peter and Paul (June 29)
Assumption of the Blessed Virgin Mary (August 15)
All Saints (November 1)

1 *Code of Canon Law*, c. 1247. All canon law quotes are from the Vatican website.

Immaculate Conception (December 8)

Christmas (December 25)

In practice, the number of obligatory holy days has varied from time to time and place to place. Individual bishops or bishops' conferences may dispense with the obligation or transfer the holy day to a Sunday if the observance is burdensome for a large number of people. The bishops are also free to *add* obligatory days, requiring locals to attend Mass for a feast that is not obligatory in the universal Church.

In the United States, the bishops have dispensed Catholics from the obligation to attend Mass on the Solemnity of Saint Joseph and the Solemnity of Saints Peter and Paul. The bishops have also moved Corpus Christi's observance from a moveable Thursday to the following Sunday. Thus, Catholics fulfill the obligation by attending Sunday Mass, which they are always required to do anyway. The Solemnity of the Epiphany is similarly transferred, in the United States, from January 6 to the Sunday after the completion of the Christmas Octave. In some dioceses, the Feast of the Ascension is also transferred from a moveable Thursday to the following Sunday.

❧

The Church uses still other designations to mark days and groups of days on the Church's calendar. In fact, the vocabulary is probably rich enough to fill a small dictionary of its own. Here we will define just a few more terms that appear often in the chapters ahead. We will provide other definitions throughout the book as the need arises.

Vigil—the eve, or day and night, before a solemnity. Some of these solemnities have their own evening Vigil Mass with special prayers and readings for use when Mass is celebrated on the evening of the day preceding the solemnity (e.g., the Vigil of Pentecost). The Mass on Saturday evening before the solemnity of Sunday is called an anticipated Mass, because the Mass readings and prayers are the same as those of Sunday. Attending Mass on the Saturday evening will fulfill the Church's obligation of attending Mass on a Sunday.

Octave—a period of eight days, beginning with one of the great feasts (for example, Christmas or Easter). The Church's liturgies celebrate all eight days as if they were the feast day, using the prayers proper to the feast.

Season—an extended period of days associated with a great solemnity, either as preparation for it or celebration of it. Advent is a season of preparation for Christmas, as Lent is for Easter. But Christmas and Easter also have seasons of their own, extending their celebration for several weeks.

Cycle—a period that commemorates and celebrates the great mysteries of Christ. The Christmas cycle includes a period of preparation, called Advent, and continues through the Christmas Season until the Feast of the Baptism of the Lord. The Easter cycle begins on Easter Vigil and continues through Pentecost.

☙❧

The Church's calendar is an intricate, complex, and beautiful technology. It is the work of many human hands and human minds trained to deal with holy things. The seasons turn and the feasts interplay like the gears in a priceless clock. They regulate our religious life and enrich our spiritual life.

They seem to happen automatically, but only because the Church oversees the apparatus, averts temporal collisions, and finely tunes all the components to make the year as festive as it can be.

CHAPTER 6

Sunday

I was in the Spirit on the Lord's day.
—Revelation 1:10

AMID THE MANY REVOLUTIONS of the twentieth century, there arose—at least among technocrats—an international movement for calendar reform. Sponsored first by the League of Nations and later by the United Nations, it was secular in origin and orientation, peevish about irregularities, and tone-deaf to religious concerns. In fact, it was religious groups that succeeded in getting the UN to table the idea indefinitely.

The Catholic Church's position was nuanced. The Second Vatican Council explicitly said that it did not "oppose efforts designed to introduce a perpetual calendar into civil society." At the same time, the Council emphasized, the Church could support only "those systems which retain and safeguard a seven-day week with Sunday."[1]

---

1 Second Vatican Council, *Sacrosanctum Concilium* (Constitution on the Sacred Liturgy), December 4, 1963, Appendix.

The Church needs Sunday. The Church requires Sunday. On behalf of the Lord and Christian people, the Church even demands Sunday.

Sunday is Christianity's "primordial feast" and the "basis and centre of the liturgical year."[2] It is the model for all other feasts, and the other feasts make little sense apart from it. If the calendar is a catechism, then Sunday is its most important lesson.

Sunday is fundamental to the Church's calendar—and, indeed, to the Church. "The Sunday Eucharist is the foundation and confirmation of all Christian practice" (CCC, 2181). As an institution, Sunday is older than some of the writings of the New Testament. It was established long before any churches were built.

It was foundational and uncontested, in fact, from the first day of redemption. Yet the Church's observance of "the Lord's Day" arose, apparently, from no command of the Lord or the apostles. It does not appear as a concern of the Council of Jerusalem (see Acts 15).

Nevertheless, the first Christians were consistent, jubilant—and adamant—about celebrating their holy day on the *first day* of the week, thus setting themselves apart from one of the most distinctive practices of their Jewish contemporaries. As faithfully as Jews kept the Sabbath, Christians celebrated the Lord's Day.

Each of the Gospels makes clear that Jesus's resurrection took place on "the first day of the week"; Saint Mark and Saint John even repeat the detail, so readers can't miss it (see Matthew 28:1; Mark 16:2, 9; Luke 24:1; and John 20:19). "And very early

---

2 Congregation for Divine Worship and the Discipline of the Sacraments, *Directory on Popular Piety and the Liturgy*, December 2001, 95.

on the first day of the week they went to the tomb when the sun
had risen" (Mark 16:2).

It was the first day of the week, and Jesus emerged from his
garden tomb—and Mary Magdalene thought he was the gar-
dener (see John 20:15). The scene is suggestive of the Garden
of Eden at the beginning of time, with Adam emerging into
new life. Thus the Gospels present the resurrection "on the first
day" as a the beginning of a new creation, a new beginning for
humanity.

On that same Sunday, Jesus appeared to two of his disciples
as they walked along the road to Emmaus. He interprets the
Scriptures for them, but they do not recognize him until he

breaks bread for them. "And their eyes were opened and they recognized him; and he vanished out of their sight. . . . he was known to them in the breaking of the bread" (Luke 24:31, 35).

The apostle Thomas missed those opportunities to see Jesus on the "first day," but Jesus caught up to him on the following Sunday, the eighth day (John 20:26).

Sunday was also the day the Lord sent his Holy Spirit upon the Church—on the first Pentecost (see Acts 2).

For the first Christians, Sunday was clearly the day when Christ appeared and gave them his Spirit. Every Sunday he was a Real Presence with the community. The Gospel accounts set the tone for the Church's liturgy in the first generation, and they have done so for every generation afterward. "On the evening of that day, the first day of the week, the doors being shut where the disciples were, for fear of the Jews, Jesus came and stood among them and said to them, 'Peace be with you'" (John 20:19).

There is a duality to the early Christian accounts. Sunday is the first day, and it is the eighth day. As the *first day,* it is the anniversary of the resurrection, and it marks the beginning of a new creation (as in Genesis 1:5). As the *eighth* day, Sunday also represents completion and even superabundance—divine grace added to a cosmos that was already "very good" (Genesis 1:31). The Lord's Day is like the Lord himself: it is the Alpha and the Omega, the beginning and the end (Revelation 21:6).

Sunday's dual nature remains with us today, even in secular society. Sunday is both the first day of the week and the last day of the weekend.

In the primitive Church we find Sunday worship as the norm (Acts 20:7). It is the day on which the community gathers and can take up a collection for the poor (1 Corinthians 16:2). It is the time when Christians worship "in the Spirit" (Revelation 1:10). It represents Easter and Pentecost as permanent features in the Church's life.

Sunday worship emerged immediately as something distinctive about the movement established by Jesus. His followers emphasized the distinction. Already in the first century we find a Christian author drawing a bright line between the Jewish Sabbath and the Christian Sunday. Identifying himself as "Barnabas," he imagines Jesus saying: "It is not your present Sabbaths that are acceptable, but the Sabbath that I have made. On that day, when I have set all things at rest, I will make the beginning of the eighth day, which is the beginning of another world." The author goes on to conclude: "This is why we keep the eighth day for rejoicing, when Jesus rose from the dead."[3]

Later in the same generation, Saint Ignatius of Antioch (in the early second century) refers to Christians as those who "no longer observe the Sabbath, but fashion their lives after the Lord's Day."[4]

In the New Testament, Saint Paul urged Christians not to cling to the ceremonial law of ancient Israel. He admonished the Galatians, for example, not to insist on the circumcision of adult converts. He warned the Colossians against the practice of Jewish dietary restrictions (Colossians 2:16). Keeping the Jewish Sabbath was seen similarly as a sign of being unable to let go of the old ways, and thus an incomplete acceptance of Jesus's new

---

3 *Letter of Barnabas*, 15.8–9.
4 Saint Ignatius of Antioch, *Letter to the Magnesians*, 9.

dispensation. The early Church held Sunday worship to be a nonnegotiable mark of Christian orthodoxy.

Sunday did not become simply a Christian version of the Sabbath. Christians were wary of enforcing a day of rest, as such enforcement had been turned on Jesus during his earthly ministry (see, for example, Mark 2:23-27). In any event, most Christians could not refrain from labor on Sunday because it was an ordinary workday in the Greco-Roman world.

Christian observance centered on the Mass, which was in most places offered very early in the morning (before work), but sometimes also in the evening (after work). Some churches offered a festive banquet every Sunday, to which Christians brought dishes to share with the community. The feast took place in conjunction with the Mass. Saint Paul seems to be talking about such a feast in his First Letter to the Corinthians (chapter 11).

By the fourth century, Sunday was firmly established, and there was little danger of Christians backsliding into observance of the Jewish ceremonial law. At this time we see a renewed appreciation of the holy day as a day of rest. In the year 321 the first Christian emperor, Constantine, enacted a law prohibiting unnecessary work on Sunday. It was the only sure way to protect the rights of the poor to worship. Even Christian taskmasters, it seems, would have made it impossible for their laborers to attend Mass if they hadn't been compelled by law to close up shop on Sundays.

❧

No one should need to be convinced of the benefits of an encounter with Jesus Christ on the terms that Jesus himself established—terms that were confirmed by the apostles and the later Church Fathers. But people do not always pursue their own best interest. Recall that God had to *command* his people to "remember the Sabbath" and enjoy a godly rest.

The Church, too, from early times, spoke of an *obligation* to attend Sunday worship. In AD 306 a Church council in Spain ruled: "If anyone who lives in the city does not attend Church services for three Sundays, let that person be expelled for a brief time in order to make the reproach public."[5]

It was, and it remains, a serious sin to miss Mass on Sunday or a holy day of obligation. We satisfy our obligation by attending Mass in a Catholic Church either on Sunday or on the evening of the preceding day (see CCC, 2180). One needs to

---

5 Council of Elvira, c. 21.

go to confession if one knowingly and willingly fails to attend Sunday Mass.

Our obligation, moreover, does not end with attendance at Mass. It includes also the savor of Sabbath leisure. The *Code of Canon Law* tells us:

> On Sundays and other holy days of obligation, the faithful are obliged to participate in the Mass.
>
> Moreover, they are to abstain from those works and affairs which hinder the worship to be rendered to God, the joy proper to the Lord's day, or the suitable relaxation of mind and body.[6]

There are times, of course, when it is impossible or inadvisable to attend Mass. When we are sick with a contagious disease, we should stay home. If we are caring for a sick family member and no one is available to relieve us, we should, of course, remain where we are needed. If we are visiting a place where there are no Catholic churches or available clergy, we are certainly excused.

Travel by itself is not an excuse. When planning a trip to an unfamiliar place, we should also research the Catholic parishes nearby and their schedules for Sunday Mass. Most of this information is readily available for churches throughout North America, but also in Europe and elsewhere. It is unlikely that we would forget to arrange lodging in advance of our journey. We should be just as diligent about lining up our Sunday Mass.

A Catholic who cannot attend Mass—for whatever reason—

---

6 *Code of Canon Law*, c. 1247.

is still obligated to observe the Lord's Day. The *Catechism* advises that we do so by making time for prayer, either alone, with family or friends, or even in groups of families (CCC, 2183).

We should be careful, too, to make every Sunday a restful day, not only for ourselves, but for others as well. We should try not to make our neighbors work unnecessarily on Sunday. The *Catechism* offers balanced, prudent advice. If we follow it, we can help to hallow the Lord's Day without falling into scrupulosity or legalism.

> Sanctifying Sundays and holy days requires a common effort. Every Christian should avoid making unnecessary demands on others that would hinder them from observing the Lord's Day. Traditional activities (sport, restaurants, etc.), and social necessities (public services, etc.), require some people to work on Sundays, but everyone should still take care to set aside sufficient time for leisure. With temperance and charity the faithful will see to it that they avoid the excesses and violence sometimes associated with popular leisure activities. In spite of economic constraints, public authorities should ensure citizens a time intended for rest and divine worship. Employers have a similar obligation toward their employees. (CCC, 2187)

৵৩

The first Christians, as Jews, had no special name for their holy day. It was simply "the first day of the week," the first day after the Jewish Sabbath. A little later they came to call it the Lord's Day, in Greek *Kyriake Hemera,* or just *Kyriake.* It is from these Greek words that we derive our English word *church.* The

Church is what assembles for Mass on the Lord's Day (in Latin, *Dies Domini*).

Many modern languages have retained this way of speaking about the first day of the week. This day is the Lord's—in Portuguese and Spanish, *Domingo;* in Italian, *Domenica;* in French, *Dimanche*.

The Romans dedicated each day to one of the gods of their pantheon. The first day was named for the sun god, Sol Invictus, the "Unconquered Sun." The day was *dies Solis,* Sun day. Thus, Saint Justin Martyr's description of the Roman Mass, set down in AD 150, begins with the words: "On the day we call the day of the sun, all who dwell in the city or country gather in the same place."[7]

Justin goes on to explain that Sunday was the normal day for the Church to perform baptisms and share the Eucharist. Baptismal fonts would eventually be made in octagonal form to suit their use on the "eighth day."

Thus the Church was born from the Lord's Day. Christians are born from the fundamental and pre-eminent feast of Jesus Christ.

---

7 CCC, 1345l; Saint Justin Martyr, *First Apology,* 65–67.

CHAPTER 7

The Solemnity of Easter

And [Jesus] said to them, "I have earnestly desired
to eat this Passover with you."
—Luke 22:15

EASTER IS THE "SOLEMNITY OF solemnities." It is not just one
feast among all the others, but the greatest feast of the Church's
year. It is the source of light for all the others and indeed for
every celebration of the Holy Mass. The Easter mystery, said
Pope Paul VI, "constitutes the essence of Christian worship
in its daily, weekly and yearly unfolding."[1] Every Sunday the
Church marks a "little Easter"; and Easter itself is Sunday writ
large.[2]

Easter is so great that it cannot be contained within a mere
twenty-four hours. The Church marks the three days leading
up to Easter as the Easter Triduum, beginning on the evening

---

1 Pope Paul VI, *Mysterii Paschalis,* introductory paragraph. See also CCC, 1168–1171.
2 "Thus the solemnity of Easter has the same kind of preeminence in the liturgical year
that Sunday has in the week." Congregation for Divine Worship, *General Norms for the
Liturgical Year and the Calendar,* February 14, 1969, 18.

THE RESURRECTION
OF OUR LORD
FROM THE DEAD

of Holy Thursday and continuing through Good Friday and Holy Saturday. On the evening of Holy Saturday, the Church officially begins the Easter feast by celebrating its vigil in a dramatic, hours-long liturgy. The Triduum shows the integral nature of all the events we commemorate in the paschal mystery:

Jesus's institution of the Eucharist, his suffering and death, and his resurrection.

From Easter Sunday, the Church carries the celebration forward to the Second Sunday of Easter, observing those eight days as if they were a single, solemn, joyful day—an "octave." The Easter Season continues for a full fifty days, concluding with Pentecost. The Church tells us: "The fifty days from Easter Sunday to Pentecost are celebrated in joyful exultation as one feast day, or better as one 'great Sunday.'"[3]

The Easter message is clear and direct: Jesus Christ is risen from the dead. What brings Catholics to church on Easter is an act of personal faith. We gather to hear, once again, the proclamation that is at the very heart of Christian faith: Christ is risen!

At the Easter Vigil, the Easter proclamation, the *Exsultet,* tells us: "Exult, let them exult . . . Be glad, let earth be glad . . . Rejoice!" Why? Because "Christ has conquered!" The proclamation goes on: "This is the night when Christ broke the prison-bars of death and rose victorious from the underworld."

For two millennia, believers have come together to celebrate Jesus's resurrection. We who are on earth today were not there in the garden, at the empty tomb, so we need to hear again the testimony of those who were. But Easter is not merely a historical commemoration. We come because we know that we, too, can share in Jesus's resurrection. At the renewal of baptismal promises on Easter Sunday, we are reminded that "through the paschal mystery we have been buried with Christ in baptism so that we may walk with him in newness of life."

The oldest records we have of the Gospel proclamation are Saint Paul's letters, and he places Jesus's resurrection at the heart

---

3 Ibid., 22.

of Christianity: "For I delivered to you as of first importance what I also received, that Christ died for our sins in accordance with the scriptures, that he was buried, that he was raised on the third day in accordance with the scriptures" (1 Corinthians 15:3-4). This is what Paul traveled the earth to communicate, to "hand on" as sacred tradition. It is a summary of the Gospel. The early Christians called it the rule and measure of faith.

Easter is so integral to the meaning of Jesus's mission that Paul describes the Lord simply as "our Passover" or "our paschal lamb" (1 Corinthians 5:7).

☙

A word of explanation is in order. As English-speakers, we are at a disadvantage when we speak of "Easter" and when we contemplate the "Easter mysteries." The word we use for the holiday is unique. It stands for the *Christian* holiday, and *only* the Christian holiday. The name in English is a relative novelty in history, so it draws our attention to all that is *new* about the feast.

That is not how most Christians in the rest of the world refer to the feast. Most other languages use the same word to describe both the Jewish holiday we know as *Passover* and the Christian holiday we know as *Easter*. Most languages describe both festivals with a word derived from the Hebrew *Pesach*. In Italy, both Jews and Christians celebrate *Pasqua;* in Spain, *Pascua;* in Sweden, *Påsk.* The same principle applies to Christians and Jews who speak Afrikaans, Albanian, Basque, Bulgarian, Danish, Dutch, Finnish, French, Greek, Icelandic, Indonesian, Khmer, Norwegian, Portuguese, Turkish, Welsh, and Zulu, among other tongues.

When most Christians speak the name of this holiday,

they evoke Jesus's continuity with the experience of ancient Israel—the deliverance from slavery in Egypt, the sparing of the firstborn children, the annual sacrifice of the lamb, the remembrance of the seder meal.

The paschal mystery encompasses the events that began with the Last Supper and culminated in the descent of the Holy Spirit upon the whole Church at Pentecost. But it is also the interpretive key for all of Jesus's earthly days—and indeed all of history leading up to his incarnation, and all of history following his ascension. We are always celebrating his Passover, but most especially on Easter.

The *Catechism of the Catholic Church* makes the connection explicitly when it refers to Easter as "the Christian Passover" (1170). In Easter, the great festival of ancient Israel—of God's deliverance of his chosen people—comes to an unexpected fulfillment in the passion, death, and resurrection of Jesus Christ. God's people are delivered from something far worse than slavery. Christ delivers them from sin and death and empowers them to live in the glorious liberty of the children of God.

Salvation is more than the lifting of a judicial sentence. Jesus Christ has taken our sins upon himself, and he has expiated our guilt. Forgiveness is indeed a tremendous grace, but it is only the beginning. God forgives our sins so that we are capable of receiving the greatest gift: the sharing of his divine life. Through the Easter sacraments—baptism, Eucharist, and confirmation—we become partakers of the divine nature. We become a *new creation* in Jesus Christ. "Therefore, if any one is

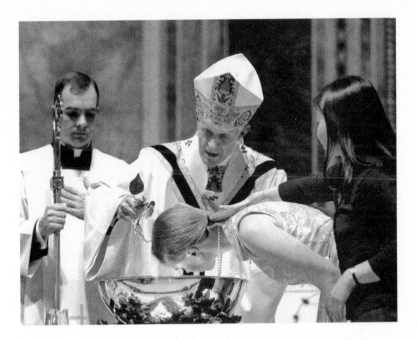

The Church receives new members through baptism at Easter Vigil.

in Christ, he is a new creation; the old has passed away, behold, the new has come" (2 Corinthians 5:17).

Easter is the wellspring of new life, because it is the wellspring of the sacraments. On Easter the Church welcomes new members through the sacraments of initiation—and renews the sacramental life of its established members. This is why the Church has traditionally imposed an "Easter Duty" on all believers, an obligation to confess their sins and make a good Communion, at some time during Lent or Easter Season. Like all obligations of the Church, it is a gentle way of bringing us into the fullness of the celebration, renewing us by means of Christ's "Passover."

The renewal of creation is symbolized richly in the Easter liturgy. The Easter Vigil employs darkness, light, fire, water, and oil—reminding us of the creation of the world, as described in the book of Genesis. It is customary to decorate the church with flowers, particularly lilies, whose pure white matches the priest's vestments and suggests so many powerful passages from Scripture:

> *My beloved has gone down to his garden,*
> *to the beds of spices,*
> *to pasture his flock in the gardens,*
> *and to gather lilies.*
> *I am my beloved's and my beloved is mine;*
> *he pastures his flock among the lilies.*
> —Song of Songs 6:2-3

Though this poem appears in the Old Testament, it has often been interpreted as an allegory of the love of Christ for his Church. Upon his death he went down to his garden tomb, where his body was prepared with ointments and spices (Mark 16:1). On Easter this Good Shepherd rose to "pasture his flock" and feed them. On Easter he still gathers the Church.

The Easter liturgy dramatically restores the two ancient songs of praise, the *Gloria* ("Glory to God in the highest") and the *Alleluia,* both of which are suppressed during the Lenten Season. *Alleluia* is the acclamation most closely associated with Easter, and that tradition draws from Passover's Jewish roots.

☙

The Easter Vigil liturgy begins with the blessing of
the Easter Candle and the fire. Light illuminates the darkness.

The word *alleluia* is a transliteration of two Hebrew words
meaning "praise the Lord" or "praise God." Since ancient times
the Hebrew *Hallelujah* has been an important part of the Passover celebration of the Jews. It is a key word in certain Psalms,
called Hallel or "Praise" Psalms. In the time of Jesus, when the
Jerusalem Temple was still standing, the assisting priests (the
Levites) would chant a group of these Psalms (113–118) con-
tinuously during the sacrifice of the Passover lambs. Families
would sing two of these Psalms (113 and 114) during the Passover meal at home. These, together, were likely the "hymn"

that Jesus and his disciples sang at the end of the Last Supper (see Matthew 26:30 and Mark 14:26). This classic expression of praise—*Alleluia!*—became an important part of the Christian celebration of the paschal Mystery.

Consider the reasons devout Jews have given for their praise. In the Talmud (from around AD 200) we can find the oldest account of the rites of the Passover meal: "In every generation a man must so regard himself as if he came forth himself out of Egypt. . . . He brought us out from bondage to freedom, from sorrow to gladness, and from mourning to a festival day, and from darkness to great light, and from servitude to redemption; so let us say before him the *Hallelujah*."[4]

What Jesus was celebrating with his apostles at the Last Supper, his definitive Passover meal, is what he continues to celebrate with the Church at every Easter—and indeed at every Mass. In this new Passover he delivers his faithful from bondage to freedom, from sorrow to gladness, from mourning to joy, from darkness to light, from slavery to redemption. That is the meaning of salvation. That is the reason the Church sings praise. And that is the reason why *Alleluia* is a song that belongs most especially to Easter.

During the Easter Season, every Mass may be ended with the acclamation, sung or recited.

Go forth, the Mass is ended. Alleluia, alleluia.
Thanks be to God. Alleluia, alleluia.

<hr />

4 Mishnah Pesahim 10.5.

Every culture has its own ways of celebrating Easter, and the holiday has accumulated many customs down the centuries. They range from the sublime to the playful.

On the sublime end, it has been common from ancient times for Christians to exchange a profound, though simple, greeting during the Easter Octave. One person says: "Christ is risen! Alleluia!" And the other replies: "Indeed he is risen! Alleluia!"

In some places, believers set out early on Easter morning in two processions, from opposite ends of town. One group marches with a statue of Jesus, and the other with a statue of Mary. When the two processions meet, the people sing Easter hymns as "the risen Christ greets his mother." There are many variations on this custom.

More purely fun are the filling of Easter baskets, the hunting of Easter eggs, and the proliferation of jelly beans. Even these help to tell the Easter story in a way. For salvation arrives as a gift that is lavish and generous, as a new life full of sweetness and beauty.

❧

Easter is a moveable feast. It is observed on different dates from year to year, because the Church always celebrates it on a Sunday close to the Jewish feast of Passover, and the Jewish calendar differs substantially from the calendar in general use today. To put it precisely: Easter falls on the Sunday after the full moon of Passover, the first full moon of spring in the Northern Hemisphere (CCC, 1170). Easter may arrive as early as March 22 or as late as April 25.

Obviously, Easter is not celebrated on an anniversary date.

In the early Church some Christians did mark the event on the actual day of Passover, the fifteenth day of the Hebrew month of Nisan. This was the common practice in Asia, and some of the great saints of that time said they had learned it from the apostle John. Christians in the West said they had been instructed by Saints Peter and Paul to celebrate Easter always on a Sunday. The Church maintained these two traditions for many years, but finally they could not bear to be divided in the celebration of the greatest Christian feast. Meeting at the Council of Nicaea in AD 325, the bishops decided to standardize the date and so established the calculations we still use today.

Unfortunately, Christians have again drifted apart on this important celebration. When most countries adopted the Gregorian calendar reform, the Orthodox churches decided to continue keeping the old Julian calendar. So the Catholic and Orthodox observances rarely line up, and sometimes the celebrations fall several weeks apart. Unifying the celebration of Easter has again become a goal of Christians. The issue was addressed at the Second Vatican Council and has been discussed by the popes since then. It is possible that the matter will be settled in years not too far ahead.

CHAPTER 8

The Solemnity of Christmas

But when the time had fully come,
God sent forth his Son, born of woman,
born under the law, to redeem those
who were under the law, so that we might
receive adoption as sons.
—Galatians 4:4-5

IF THE CHURCH YEAR COULD be read by a compass, Easter would be "magnetic north"—the standard point of reference because "the Paschal Mystery and its celebration constitutes the essence of Christian worship in its daily, weekly and yearly unfolding."[1]

Just as surely, though, the opposite pole would be Christmas. Jesus Christ came into the world for the sake of our salvation, so Christmas—like all the other feasts—is ordered to Easter. But it's just as true to say that the Easter mysteries are possible only because the Word became flesh and made his dwelling among us, so Easter depends on and presupposes Christmas.

---

1 Pope Paul VI, *Mysterii Paschalis,* introductory paragraph.

Scholars thrive on debate, and theologians in particular like to argue about the relative weight of the two great holy days. Cardinal Christoph Schönborn, the archbishop of Vienna and the primary editor of the *Catechism of the Catholic Church,* summarizes the conversation, which has been going on for centuries:

> If, on the one hand, we start from the Incarnation, when God became man, then it seems to follow that Christmas is the central saving event: God became man! With that, everything has already been fulfilled. Yet is Easter then any more than an appendix? Have redemption and salvation not come to us already, before Easter? On the other hand, Christ's Paschal Mystery does nonetheless seem to be central: Easter is the turning point of salvation, the new thing that makes everything new. Is Easter the noun, then, and Christmas merely the preposition? . . . Yet in fact the two belong together, each unthinkable without the other.[2]

Easter and Christmas are the two great points of the Church year. Each is preceded by a long season of preparation, Easter by Lent and Christmas by Advent. And each is followed by a long season of celebration, an abiding "Day of the Lord": the Easter Season, the Christmas Season. Each has its great vigil. Each has gathered, down the millennia, many ritual traditions and ethnic customs. Each has its own particular ambience, its characteristic message, and its own distinctive joy.

2 Christoph Cardinal Schönborn, *God Sent His Son: A Contemporary Christology* (San Francisco: Ignatius Press, 2010), 65. Cf. Donald Cardinal Wuerl, *Faith that Transforms Us: Reflections on the Creed* (Frederick, Md.: Word Among Us Press, 2013), 58.

We need not make the case for the cultural and commercial importance of Christmas. Entire industries—toys, jewelry, movies—stake their success on it and forecast their sales by it. Economists and stockbrokers watch the seasonal signs almost as closely as the magi did (see Matthew 2:1-2).

Christmas is a fixture in the civilization. It is institutionalized generosity. It looks almost like a religion of its own, with its own canon of readings (such as Charles Dickens's *A Christmas Carol*); its own songs for radio play; and its own mythic movies, from *Miracle on 34th Street* to *A Charlie Brown Christmas*. Because Western civilization is built on Christian foundations, Christmas is an institution with sacred and secular significance, marked by Christians and non-Christians.

Many people would prefer that the holiday drop its sacred associations altogether, so that the day could be given over entirely to eating and drinking and accumulating more stuff. In the city where we spent our youth, the town fathers once tried to de-christen the day and rename it "Sparkle Season," a name that (theoretically, at least) would not offend non-Christians. The ploy backfired, as the Christian majority found the *new name* offensive, and just about everyone found the name silly.

When we try to remove Christ from Christmas, what are we left with? Bills from overspending, anxiety over pointless social events, and a big letdown on December 26 or thereabouts.

The sacred season, on the other hand, inspires giving as a *selfless* act, and it moderates our emotions by means of Advent's preparation and then the Christmas Season's gradual denouement.

Christmas provides a divine model for generosity. It can indeed inspire us to extravagance, if we're inclined that way. But

Jesus is the reason for our giving, and he can keep us reasonable. Saint Paul suggests that the holiday should lead us to be Christ-like in our giving.

> Have this mind among yourselves, which was in Christ Jesus, who, though he was in the form of God, did not count equality with God a thing to be grasped, but emptied himself, taking the form of a servant, being born in the likeness of men. (Philippians 2:5-7)

That's generosity. Christ left heaven to spend his days with us. That, as the hackneyed saying goes, is the true meaning of Christmas. That's what we need to imitate: a love that is giving and not grasping.

Yet Saint Paul doesn't leave his meditation at Christmas; he proceeds in the next verse to the paschal mystery, to Easter: "And being found in human form he humbled himself and became obedient unto death, even death on a cross. Therefore God has highly exalted him" (Philippians 2:8-9).

Christmas is never far from Easter. Indeed, as Cardinal Schönborn put it, each is unthinkable without the other. Christ came to live with us. He came to die for us, so that we might rise with him.

༺༻

Christ came at a particular moment of history. His story does not begin "Once upon a time" or "A long time ago in a galaxy far, far away." His story begins with minute historical detail. Here is Saint Luke's account:

In those days a decree went out from Caesar Augustus that all the world should be enrolled. This was the first enrollment, when Quirinius was governor of Syria. And all went to be enrolled, each to his own city. And Joseph also went up from Galilee, from the city of Nazareth, to Judea, to the city of David, which is called Bethlehem, because he was of the house and lineage of David, to be enrolled with Mary, his betrothed, who was with child. And while they were there, the time came for her to be delivered. And she gave birth to her first-born son and wrapped him in swaddling cloths, and laid him in a manger, because there was no place for them in the inn. (Luke 2:1-7)

In the space of a few lines we learn that the birth of Jesus took place in a particular place at a specific time. We find out the names of the rulers during that period. We learn a bit about the ancestry of the main characters. In the verses that follow, Saint Luke brings in the testimony of other witnesses.

This is history—"real history," as Pope Benedict XVI said in the last volume of his series entitled Jesus of Nazareth.[3]

Salvation came not because God hovered above the earth in a vaguely spiritual way. Salvation came when the Word took flesh and was born of flesh at an identifiable time in a place you can still visit. The Church announces this in vivid terms in its traditional and poetic "Proclamation of the Birth of Christ," which may be chanted at Midnight Mass on Christmas Eve.

The Twenty-fifth Day of December,

when ages beyond number had run their course
from the creation of the world,

---

3 Pope Benedict XVI, *Jesus of Nazareth: The Infancy Narratives* (New York: Image, 2012), 17.

when God in the beginning created heaven and earth,
and formed man in his own likeness;

when century upon century had passed
since the Almighty set his bow in the clouds after the Great
    Flood,
as a sign of covenant and peace;

in the twenty-first century since Abraham, our father in faith,
came out of Ur of the Chaldees;

in the thirteenth century since the People of Israel were led by
    Moses

in the Exodus from Egypt;

around the thousandth year since David was anointed King;

in the sixty-fifth week of the prophecy of Daniel;

in the one hundred and ninety-fourth Olympiad;

in the year seven hundred and fifty-two
since the foundation of the City of Rome;

in the forty-second year of the reign of Caesar Octavian Augustus,

the whole world being at peace,

JESUS CHRIST, eternal God and Son of the eternal
    Father,

desiring to consecrate the world by his most loving presence,
was conceived by the Holy Spirit,
and when nine months had passed since his conception,
was born of the Virgin Mary in Bethlehem of Judah,
and was made man:

The Nativity of Our Lord Jesus Christ according to the flesh.

We do not say that December 25 is the indisputably accurate anniversary date—though tradition advances a respectable case for it. Nor do we say that Christians have counted the years correctly since Jesus was born. In fact, we know that we've miscounted. A monk in the sixth century named Dennis the Little made a miscalculation and missed the year of Jesus's birth by four to six years.

What we celebrate is the historical fact of the incarnation and the public appearance of the eternal Son of God as Jesus of Nazareth. What we celebrate is our salvation.

၏ဗ

Christmas is a contraction for "Christ's Mass," and like all the feasts it is a summons to worship. It is a holy day of obligation. We must not fail to attend the Christ's Mass.

We hear the summons at the beginning of so many Christmas liturgies. Perhaps the most common processional hymn is the English translation of the Latin hymn "Adeste Fideles."

O come all ye faithful, joyful and triumphant!
O come ye, O come ye, to Bethlehem

This is the time the Church gathers to celebrate the birth of Christ. Time falls away as we worship, and in our hearts we find ourselves worshiping at the place where the Word was made flesh and appeared before us. Pope Pius XII wrote: "With the coming of the birthday of the Redeemer, [the Church] would bring us to the cave of Bethlehem and there teach that we must be born again and undergo a complete reformation; that will only happen when we are intimately and vitally united to the Word of God made man and participate in His divine nature, to which we have been elevated."[4]

A Christian of the second century said: "The Word of God became man, that you may learn from man how man may become God."[5] Through the feast of Christmas, God shows humanity how to become his children—through the humility, the generosity, and the charity of the newborn Jesus.

One reason we associate gift giving with Christmas is because this feast marks the time of God's greatest gift. He sent his only begotten Son to become one of us, to be with us. Because he gave, we give too, and thus we become more like him; we become more godly. We learn to give as we go "to Bethlehem" in our worship.

The very name Bethlehem suggests our way of worship. It is Hebrew for "house of bread." So we honor the "bread of life" (John 6:35) on his birthday, and we honor him "in the breaking of the bread" (Luke 24:35). There can be no more fitting way to celebrate the Christ's Mass—Christmas.

---

4 Pope Pius XII, *Mediator Dei* (encyclical on the Sacred Liturgy) November 20, 1947, 155.

5 Saint Clement of Alexandria, *Exhortation to the Heathen*, 1.

Posada, a Latin American celebration, recalls Saint Joseph's search for
lodging on the night of Jesus's birth.

The ancient Church celebrated a feast in honor of the birth of
Jesus. The date varied from place to place, but some churches
kept the feast on December 25. That is the date favored by Saint
Clement of Alexandria (Egypt), who wrote in the late second
century. Just a few years later, Saint Hippolytus of Rome cor-
roborated that date, as did Julius Africanus, who had traveled
widely and knew the practice of many far-flung churches. Still,
we know that some Christians observed March 28 as the Lord's
birthday, and others April 2, April 19, or May 20.

In the fourth century there was a movement to standardize
the feast. It gained momentum because certain heretics, called
Arians after their founder Arius, were arguing that Jesus was *not*

divine at his birth but *became* divine by adoption at his baptism. The Church wanted to issue a firm response and teach Jesus's divinity in the clearest and most memorable way—and there is no more effective way to convey doctrine than by establishing a feast.

Paying homage to the newborn Jesus at the blessing of a creche.

Some historians believe that the Church also wanted to counteract a pagan festival that had grown immensely popular, that of the Unconquered Sun, also held on December 25 because of its proximity to the winter solstice.

As early as AD 336 the Church of Rome took up the promotion of Christmas on December 25, and other churches soon followed. Saint John Chrysostom was a great advocate for the feast in the Eastern churches. By the end of the fourth century, many of the major Christian figures in the world were advocating the celebration of the feast on December 25.

☙☙

In the weeks that follow Christmas—the week at the end of the secular calendar, and the weeks beginning the new year—the Church continues to celebrate the Christmas Season. The readings at Mass commemorate Jesus's birth and early manifestations—his appearance to the magi, his presentation in the Temple, and the flight into Egypt to escape King Herod's wrath.

Christmas, like Easter, has an octave: eight days that are celebrated as one day. The Sunday within the Christmas Octave is the Feast of the Holy Family. Within Christmas Season there are many other important days: the Solemnities of Mary Mother of God (January 1) and the Feast of the Epiphany (January 6), the Feast of Saint Stephen, the first martyr (December 26), the Feast of Saint John the Apostle (December 27), and the Feast of the Holy Innocents who were slaughtered by Herod in their infancy (December 28).

Christmas Season ends on the Sunday falling after January 6, the Feast of the Baptism of the Lord. Yet in a sense it never ends: at every Mass we experience the Word made flesh, dwelling among us. In the Catholic Church, the "feast" of the Lord's incarnation—like the generous spirit of Christmas—is always in season.

CHAPTER 9

The Solemnity of Pentecost

*When the day of Pentecost had come, they were all together
in one place.*
—Acts 2:1

PENTECOST IS AN EXOTIC-SOUNDING WORD to those of us
who speak English, and we associate it with extraordinary things.
"Pentecostal" is an adjective used to describe ecstatic and even
mystical experiences—events that are by definition unusual.

Yet the word in its original Greek could not be more workaday and ordinary. It means "fiftieth." For Jews, Pentecost is the
"fiftieth" day at the end of the seven weeks following Passover.
(In Hebrew it is called Shavuot which means "Weeks"; it is
forty-nine days between Passover and Pentecost, that is, seven
sevens, a week of weeks.) Among the Jews in ancient times, the
holiday served a dual purpose: it was a harvest festival, and it
celebrated the giving of the Law to Moses. The fields were just
beginning to ripen, so the people offered their "first fruits" to
God. The rabbis connected this feast with the Law because the
book of Exodus (19:1) indicates that the Israelites entered the

wilderness of Sinai, where they received the commandments, on the third new moon after they had left Egypt.

Thus in the Old Testament, Pentecost represented a certain fruition or fulfillment of the Passover drama that began the Exodus. Liberated from slavery, the Israelites were free to worship and serve the Lord God in the way he revealed to them through his law.

Even more so in the New Testament, the first Christian Pentecost fulfilled the divine initiative begun with Jesus's paschal mystery.

Pentecost was the fiftieth day after Passover for the Jews. It was a pilgrim feast in ancient times; so Jesus's disciples, who were devout Jews, were "all together in one place" in Jerusalem to celebrate. At this first Pentecost after Jesus's resurrection, the Holy Spirit was given to the Church in a dramatic way.

> And suddenly a sound came from heaven like the rush of a mighty wind, and it filled all the house where they were sitting. And there appeared to them tongues as of fire, distributed and resting on each one of them. And they were all filled with the Holy Spirit and began to speak in other tongues, as the Spirit gave them utterance.

> Now there were dwelling in Jerusalem Jews, devout men from every nation under heaven. And at this sound the multitude came together, and they were bewildered, because each one heard them speaking in his own language. And they were amazed. . . .

> . . . and there were added that day about three thousand souls. (Acts 2:2-7, 41)

This is the event that Christians commemorate on Pentecost. It is traditionally marked as "the birthday of the Church."

From the beginning of his ministry, Jesus had made clear that his purpose was to give the Holy Spirit as a gift to his disciples. At his baptism, Jesus was identified as "he who baptizes with the Holy Spirit" (John 1:33); and Jesus himself said that baptism in the Spirit is a requirement for life in the kingdom of God (see John 3:5). Jesus would baptize with the Spirit, yet we know that in his earthly ministry "Jesus himself did not baptize, but only his disciples" (John 4:2).

The Spirit was still to come. Even as Jesus went about preaching and performing miracles, "as yet the Spirit had not been given, because Jesus was not yet glorified" (John 7:39). Jesus foretold a day when God would send the Spirit of Truth to dwell within believers (see John 14:16-17). The Spirit, Jesus told his apostles, "will teach you all things, and bring to your remembrance all that I have said to you" (John 14:26). The Spirit would give the Church its authority and give believers every good gift (see John 15:26 and 16:13-15). The Church would share the divine Gift through the sacraments, through which Christians become "partakers of the Holy Spirit" (Hebrews 6:4).

All of this was manifest on the first Pentecost. But it is not a day that passed and is gone. In the Church we live in that day for the remainder of human history. Pentecost, the *Catechism* tells us, is the beginning of a new age when Christ lives and acts in his Church (CCC, 1076).

Still, we celebrate this truth in a special way as we commemorate its inaugural event, on the Solemnity of Pentecost.

☙❧

On the day of Pentecost when the seven weeks of Easter had come to an end, Christ's Passover is fulfilled in the outpouring of the Holy Spirit, manifested, given, and communicated as a divine person: of his fullness, Christ, the Lord, pours out the Spirit in abundance. (CCC, 731)

The gift given at Pentecost was not another created good. The gift was uncreated God. Pentecost represents the full revelation of the Blessed Trinity (see CCC, 732). God the Son became man so that he could reveal the Father. On Pentecost the

Father and the Son sent the Spirit upon the Church, manifesting the Trinity.

Pentecost is a supreme moment of divine revelation, but God does not simply give information. He gives his life. He gives himself as a gift. The Holy Spirit comes to teach the Church, but from within—he lives in the Church and remains the Church's infinite and eternal source of life.

Pentecost is the Church's feast of the Holy Spirit—and it is the Church's feast of the Church. It marks a moment of transformation. After Jesus's crucifixion, the apostles had been apprehensive and a little fearful. They lacked confidence. They stayed indoors. After forty days, when Jesus ascended to glory, he promised them: "But you shall receive power when the Holy Spirit has come upon you; and you shall be my witnesses . . . to the end of the earth" (Acts 1:8).

Then, on the fiftieth day, came the outpouring of the Spirit, and with the Spirit came a certain boldness. The timid, shy, awkward, and fearful disciples suddenly became enterprising, courageous, bold proclaimers of the Gospel. Their doubts vanished. Courage filled their hearts. Prompted by the Spirit, they stepped forward and boldly proclaimed the words of Jesus.

What caused this transformation? It was the outpouring of God's Spirit on the Church—on those very apostles whom Christ had appointed to be the foundation of his Church.

Again, that outpouring of the Spirit—Pentecost—did not just happen once. The Church today continues to share in the outpouring of the Spirit, and all believers receive the same power to overcome doubt, timidity, and even fear in their efforts to accomplish whatever the Spirit asks.

One of the great biblical scholars of the early Church, a man named Origen of Alexandria, said that the true Christian "is always living in the season of Pentecost."[1]

☙☙

Catholics throughout the world observe the feast of Pentecost with many beautiful customs. Some churches drop red rose petals over their congregation to represent the descent of the Holy Spirit.

Many people look to the nine-day period between Ascension Thursday and Pentecost Sunday as the origin of the custom of praying a novena. (A novena is a form of devotion consisting of nine days of special prayers.) The New Testament tells us that the apostles secluded themselves in those days after the ascension of the Lord: "All these with one accord devoted themselves to prayer, together with the women and Mary the mother of Jesus, and with his brethren" (Acts 1:14). Their days of prayer, in the company of the Blessed Virgin, concluded with the best possible outcome: God lavished his life upon them and upon the world!

In imitation of the apostles—and in anticipation of the same divine Gift—many Catholics pray a nine-day "Novena to the Holy Spirit" between the two solemnities, Ascension and Pentecost. A popular devotion, it takes many forms, from the repetition of simple one-line aspirations, like "Come, Holy Spirit," to much more elaborate prayers on a variety of themes.

The Church encourages Catholics to pray for Christian unity in a special way during the "Pentecost Novena."[2] Why? In Saint Luke's description of the original Pentecost, the evan-

---

1 Origen, *Contra Celsum* 8.22.
2 Congregation for Divine Worship, *Directory on Popular Piety and the Liturgy*, 155.

gelist emphasizes the Church's universality—its catholicity. From the beginning, the Church was diverse and multicultural. The gathering that day included "devout men from every nation under heaven" (Acts 2:5).

> Parthians and Medes and Elamites and residents of Mesopotamia, Judea and Cappadocia, Pontus and Asia, Phrygia and Pamphylia, Egypt and the parts of Libya belonging to Cyrene, and visitors from Rome, both Jews and proselytes, Cretans and Arabians, we hear them telling in our own tongues the mighty works of God. (Acts 2:9-11)

The Spirit descended not upon a single race or tribe or nation, but upon a Church that will always be universal in its reach, united in its constitution. National boundaries do not divide believers. Nor does language or ancestry. "I believe in the Holy Spirit," we profess in the Creed every Sunday, and so "I believe in one, holy, catholic and apostolic Church."

The Church is alive in the Spirit and always living in Pentecost.

The Holy Spirit enlivens our commitment as we seek to rediscover the overwhelming truths expressed in the Creed. The Spirit strengthens us as we entrust ourselves to the life of grace and virtue promised in the sacraments. The Spirit bolsters our confidence as we open the deeper places of our heart so that his gifts might strengthen us to live our faith.

In our day-to-day lives we can depend on the Holy Spirit to come to our aid as we do our part to share the faith with others. The Holy Spirit—in urging us to begin, without hesitation, this conversation with our neighbors—will provide us openings, coaxing us to initiate the invitation, to invite our neighbors to come to Mass, to encourage them to come to Bible study or a small faith group, to ask them to consider discussing what might keep them away. People who know nothing of the faith can't come to the faith unless someone tells them about it—gives them the information they need to make a decision for God.

The Holy Spirit invites us to speak about our Catholic faith, to have the courageous, and sometimes awkward, conversation. He even wants us to reach out and invite others by name, with a smile and a friendly welcome.[3]

---

3 Cf. Cardinal Donald Wuerl, *Disciples of the Lord: Sharing the Vision: A Pastoral Letter on the New Evangelization* (Washington, D.C.: Archdiocese of Washington, 2010).

CHAPTER 10

The Solemnity of Epiphany and the Feast of the Baptism of the Lord

Great indeed, we confess, is the mystery of our religion:
He was manifested in the flesh . . .
preached among the nations,
believed on in the world,
taken up in glory.
—1 Timothy 3:16

EPIPHANY IS THE FEAST THAT celebrates the manifestation of the newborn Christ as Savior of the world. The root meaning of *epiphany* is "a sudden, dramatic appearance or perception."

In the Western Church, in modern times, we associate Epiphany especially with the adoration of Jesus by the wise men (*magi*) from the East.

Now when Jesus was born in Bethlehem of Judea in the days of Herod the king, behold, wise men from the East came to Jerusalem, saying, "Where is he who has been born king of the Jews? For we have seen his star in the East, and have come to worship him." . . .

. . . and lo, the star which they had seen in the East went before them, till it came to rest over the place where the child was. When they saw the star, they rejoiced exceedingly with great joy; and going into the house they saw the child with Mary his mother, and they fell down and worshiped him. Then, opening their treasures, they offered him gifts, gold and frankincense and myrrh. (Matthew 2:1-2, 9-11)

The magi adore the infant Jesus.

Through history and throughout the world, the feast has been celebrated in many different ways. In much of the world its cultural importance is greater than that of Christmas.

The Solemnity of Epiphany arrives at the end of the "Twelve Days of Christmas." It is traditional in many parts of the world to mark these days with great festivity, and fasting is forbidden. Families and friends exchange gifts. The magi (or three kings) fulfill the gift-giving role played by Santa Claus (Saint Nicholas) in other countries.

The traditional date of Epiphany is January 6, though the bishops in many countries have transferred the observance to the Sunday that falls between January 2 and January 8 (inclusive).

Why is Epiphany so important? Because it commemorates the public revelation that Jesus had come as Savior not only to the chosen people, the Jews, but to all the peoples of the world.

The magi came from "the East." They were gentiles—that is, non-Jews—and as pagan astrologers they were practitioners of an idolatry that was condemned in the Law of Moses. Yet God saw that they were seeking a higher wisdom, so he called them from afar to find salvation. As they approached the child and his mother, they represented all the peoples of the world. They received the Good News, the Gospel, on our behalf. In the early centuries of Christianity, believers were still surrounded by pagan religion, the pre-Christian temples with their smoky sacrifices to the gods; they were also daily witnesses to pre-Christian morality, so they saw vividly the life from which they had been saved. Epiphany was their celebration of that salvation.

Through the centuries, Epipany has represented not only Jesus's appearance to the magi, but also his other "manifestations," his other "epiphanies," especially his baptism in the Jordan and his first miracle at the wedding feast of Cana (see John 2:1-11). These events were also public "debuts" of Jesus's mission. At his baptism, the Father's voice thundered from the sky, and the Spirit descended on Jesus as a dove (see Luke 3:22).

At Cana, Jesus's miracle "manifested his glory; and his disciples believed in him" (John 2:11).

Chocolate in gold foil is a sweet way to recall the gifts of the magi on the Solemnity of Epiphany.

These were sudden, dramatic, public revelations of Jesus's divine power, and all who witnessed them were amazed. They would never forget those astonishing moments: "the life was made manifest, and we saw it, and testify to it, and proclaim to you the eternal life which was with the Father and was made manifest to us" (1 John 1:2). Nevertheless, these miracles could have been interpreted as special revelations for God's chosen people, the Jews.

The visit of the magi shows us otherwise, because in this occurrence we encounter the Good News as it would later be proclaimed by Saint Paul: "salvation has come to the Gentiles" (Romans 11:11).

Epiphany is a teaching moment, and there are good doctrinal reasons that the Church chooses to focus on the visit of the magi. Yes, it emphasizes the salvation of non-Jews, but it also emphasizes Jesus's divinity. The magi came to Jesus *and worshiped him*. They recognized him as God incarnate, even though he was just a baby.

Very early in the history of Christianity, the Church found itself combating a heresy called "adoptionism." The belief took many forms, but its basic contention was this: Jesus was not born divine; rather he *became* divine when God *adopted* him at his baptism.

The episode of the magi exposes the error of adoptionism, and the celebration of the feast makes the matter abundantly clear in the Church and to the world. Jesus Christ is, from the moment of his conception, true God and true man.

Epiphany represents a completion of the Christmas story. Christ first appeared to the people of Israel and to angels, but then he drew all the world to himself.

The baptism of the Lord is also an important revelatory moment in Jesus's life, and the Church has given it a feast all its own, on the Sunday following January 6.

Jesus's baptism marks the beginning of his public life. Saint John the Baptizer proclaimed Jesus as the Christ, the Messiah, and God himself confirmed the message in an extraordinary way, by a manifestation of the Blessed Trinity: the Father's voice, the Son's body, and the Spirit descending as a dove.

This is the moment of Jesus's anointing as priest, prophet, and king. Thus it is the end of his "hidden life," and it is the end of the Christmas Season and the beginning of a new phase of the Church's year.

The early Church saw the day as a celebration of not only the Lord's baptism, but every Christian's baptism. As a celebration of the new life that is shared through the sacrament. The Church Fathers taught that Jesus, by his immersion in the waters of the Jordan, sanctified all the waters of the earth—giving them the power to bestow divine life on human beings through baptism.

Jesus's baptism is often depicted near a church's baptismal font.
Every baby's baptism recalls the Lord's.

It is true: this most ordinary earthly element is the only material required for a valid baptism, for a new birth of a heavenly order.

For those who see with the eyes of faith, every baptism is a dramatic and sudden manifestation of God's power. It is a reason for celebration, a reason for a feast.

Seen together, the Solemnity of Epiphany and the Feast of the Baptism of the Lord are not about passivity. They are not simply feasts about graces received from God. They are also about our correspondence to those graces, our use of those gifts, in imitation of Jesus Christ. As we have received, so we give in turn.

The Gospel tells us that the star led the way for the magi. We are supposed to be a part of a great constellation of stars that light the way and show the path to others as we point to Christ in our actions and our words. Just as the star shone in the sky, pointing the way to those who sought the king and the new kingdom, so our faith sheds light on the human condition and helps modern magi, modern seekers, to sort out what truly manifests God's plan

We Christians in the modern age have too often allowed the culture to mute our participation in the public conversation about issues of personal morality and social justice.

These feasts call every member of the Church to be a light, to manifest the Gospel, to be an epiphany of Christ, a sign of all that the Church proclaims and teaches as truth.

CHAPTER 11

The Solemnity of the Ascension

No one has ascended into heaven
but he who descended from heaven,
the Son of Man.
—John 3:13

BY HIS ASCENSION INTO HEAVEN, Jesus made possible the celebration of all the feasts of the Church. For the Church celebrates the feasts liturgically—ritually—led by Jesus, the eternal priest. It is precisely at his ascension that Jesus inaugurated this new priestly order. The *Catechism* explains this well, drawing especially from the New Testament letter to the Hebrews:

> Jesus Christ, the one priest of the new and eternal Covenant, "entered, not into a sanctuary made by human hands . . . but into heaven itself, now to appear in the presence of God on our behalf" (Heb 9:24). There Christ permanently exercises his priesthood, for he "always lives to make intercession" for "those who draw near to God through him" (Heb 7:25). As "high priest of the good

things to come" he is the center and the principal actor of the liturgy that honors the Father in heaven (Heb 9:11; cf. Rev 4:6-11). (CCC, 662)

In all the Church's earthly celebrations we share in the heavenly celebration of Christ, our high priest. In the Old Testament, the priests of Israel sang "Songs of Ascent" as they climbed the steps to offer sacrifice in the Temple. The New Testament shows Jesus in his ascension as a priest entering the ultimate sanctuary—yet also as a king ascending to his throne on high. In this action, Jesus shows himself to be the "son of David" (see Matthew 1:1), for David served Israel as both priest and king.

The Solemnity of the Ascension commemorates an event recorded in the Gospels and in the Acts of the Apostles. It marks the final act of Jesus's earthly ministry (see Mark 16:15-20), and the necessary prelude to the birth of the Church (see Acts 1:6-11). Jesus ascended in his visible body to make way for his Mystical Body, the Church. In his ascension, Jesus turned over to the Church the work that he had come to do. The Church would bring salvation and healing by means of the sacraments, and the Church would preach the Good News to a world that needed (and still needs) to hear it.

As he ascended, Jesus set his apostles an ambitious task: "Go into all the world and preach the gospel to the whole creation" (Mark 16:15). And when he had disappeared into the clouds, the angels told the apostles to quit standing there and looking to heaven, and instead get on with their work.

It is a work for which they had been well prepared. The Bible tells us that Jesus spent the forty days after his resurrection instructing his disciples about the kingdom of God, so the Church traditionally observes the Solemnity of the Ascension on the fortieth day after Easter Sunday, Ascension Thursday. It is a holy day of obligation. (In some places, the solemnity has been transferred to the Seventh Sunday of Easter, and there the obligation is fulfilled by the usual Sunday Mass attendance.)

On the Solemnity of the Ascension we celebrate the glorification of Christ, the completion of his work, but also our own share in his work—and our willingness to take it up.

The forty days leading up to the feast have their own significance. Forty is an important number in the Bible. It signifies a period of preparation and purification. In the time of Noah, the rains fell for forty days to flood the earth. In the time of Moses, the tribes wandered in the desert for forty years before entering the Promised Land. Jesus fasted for forty days in preparation for his public ministry. With these precedents in mind, we can see that Jesus was preparing the apostles for something momentous by instructing them about the kingdom of God (Acts 1:3).

The early Church took note of this and set aside those forty days, between Easter and the Ascension, as a period of intense doctrinal formation, especially for new converts. In modern times, the Church has recovered this practice by restoring the mystagogy phase of the Rite of Christian Initiation for Adults. Mystagogy is an instruction in the "mysteries" of Christianity and the sacraments of the Church. It is a crucial training for Christian life on earth. Jesus "was lifted up, and a cloud took him out of their sight" (Acts 1:9). Now Christians in the world, like those first disciples, are to be witnesses to everything that has been revealed to them.

On the Ascension, the Church marks a unique event in all of history. Only Christ has gone to heaven by his own power. Only God *could* do this. As he descended to earth by the power of the Holy Spirit, so Christ returned to heavenly glory by the same divine power, symbolized by the cloud. Other biblical figures were taken to heaven, body and soul. Elijah "went up by a whirlwind" (2 Kings 2:11). Enoch "was taken up" (Hebrews 11:5) because "God took him" (Genesis 5:24). The Church teaches that the Blessed Virgin Mary, too, entered heaven at the end of her earthly days (see Revelation 12:1). All of these people were *assumed* into heaven by the power of God; but "no one has *ascended* into heaven but he who descended from heaven, the Son of man" (John 3:13).

Jesus knew that he must go before us into heaven, and he prepared his apostles for what would happen in many ways. He told them plainly: "I go to the Father, and you will see me no more" (John 16:10). On another occasion he asked: "What if you were to see the Son of man ascending where he was before?" (John 6:62). After rising from the dead, he told Mary Magdalene not to cling to him, "for I have not yet ascended to the Father" (John 20:17). Thus he foretold that his ascension would be the *precondition* of a lasting communion between himself and his people. In the Church, by means of the sacraments, we still cling to him today.

With Jesus, our humanity—our human nature, our human flesh—has entered definitively into divine glory. By the grace of the sacraments, we are partakers of his divine nature, and we believe that we shall share God's life intimately in heaven, as Jesus does. Every Christian has good reason to say, as Job did: "from my flesh I shall see God" (Job 19:26).

That is a promise worth celebrating, as we do in the Church every year on the Solemnity of the Ascension.

CHAPTER 12

The Solemnity of the Body and Blood of Christ

*The bread which I shall give for the life of
the world is my flesh.*
—John 6:51

THE SOLEMNITY OF THE BODY and Blood of Christ—
commonly known by its old Latin name, Corpus Christi—is
perhaps the most picturesque of Catholic feasts.

On this day the Church celebrates Jesus's Real Presence in
the Holy Eucharist. The feast is traditionally observed on the
Thursday after Trinity Sunday. In the United States and some
other countries, it has been assigned to the following Sunday.

Jesus said of the Eucharist: "This is my body" (Luke 22:19).
And also: "the bread which I shall give for the life of the world is
my flesh" (John 6:51). Since the first generation of the Church,
Catholics have taken the Lord at his word. They love the Eucharist, and they find creative ways to express their love in customs associated with Corpus Christi.

Carrying the monstrance in a Corpus Christi procession.

Through the urban streets of Washington, D.C., and through the pathways of remote mountain villages, parishioners carry the Blessed Sacrament—exposed in a vessel called the monstrance—in solemn procession. Sometimes they sing hymns as they go. Sometimes they are accompanied by musical instruments.

In Genzano, a hill town south of Rome, the people have for centuries carpeted the streets with artful designs made of flower petals to honor the coming of Christ in the procession.

In the Pennsylvania town of Tarentum, the people shape elaborate images in colored sawdust to decorate the pavement where Jesus passes.

Great artists and sensitive souls have been profoundly moved—and their lives changed—by the sight of a Corpus Christi procession.

The American novelist William Dean Howells never got over witnessing many thousands of parishioners from Venice's hundred churches as they moved through the city's plaza over the course of hours. He remembered it in many of his writings throughout his lifetime. Every year on Corpus Christ, the novelist Edith Wharton opened the garden of her chateau to the local parish so that the people would have a proper place to celebrate—and she could marvel at the spectacle. Neither Howells nor Wharton was Catholic.

In the late eighteenth century, Elizabeth Bayley Seton, a wealthy American of conventional Protestant piety, witnessed a Corpus Christi procession in Italy and felt that she was driven to her knees by an unseen force. She knew at that moment that she had seen the King of Kings. It was a turning point in the long drama of her conversion—a story that concludes in her canonization as a saint by the Catholic Church.

ॐ

The calendar, as we have said, is a catechism, and many historians see the feast of Corpus Christi as the Church's response to the heretical doctrine of certain wayward theologians who disbelieved Jesus's Real Presence in the Eucharist. The most notorious of these was Berengarius, a French monk of the eleventh century, who argued that the bread and wine undergo no conversion during the Mass, but that the body and blood of Christ are nonetheless mysteriously present somehow. As such heresies gained ground, faithful Catholics grew more fervent in their opposition, and they pursued more ardently the devotions cast off by the heretics.

The Dominican order, founded in the early thirteenth century, promoted eucharistic devotion, and its theologians answered the heretics' objections with reasons grounded in Scripture and good sense. The greatest voice in this movement was Saint Thomas Aquinas.

In the midthirteenth century, in Mont Cornillon, Belgium, lived a Cistercian nun named Juliana (now venerated as a saint), who was especially devoted to the Blessed Sacrament. Once while praying she saw a vision of a full moon, radiant but for one black spot. Later, in a dream, Our Lord appeared to her and explained the figures: The moon was his Church, which would be incomplete (thus the black spot) as long as it marked no feast in honor of the sacrament of his body. Juliana reported the vision to her superiors, and eventually the story made its way to her bishop, who ordered the feast to be observed locally.

Shortly after Juliana's death in 1258, a priest from her diocese was elected pope. As Urban IV, he extended the feast of Corpus Christi to the entire Latin Church. In a truly inspired moment, he assigned Thomas Aquinas to compose the poems and sequence for the liturgy. Out of that body of work came some of the most beloved hymns in the Catholic tradition: "Panis Angelicus," "Pange Lingua Gloriosi," "Tantum Ergo" (which is part of the "Pange Lingua"), and "O Salutaris Hostia." Aquinas's Corpus Christi hymns have been set to music by great composers, from César Franck to Dave Brubeck. They have been translated into English verse by major poets, from Richard Crashaw to Gerard Manley Hopkins. The original hymns continue, almost a millennium later, to be the favored playlist for the feast day.

Beauty inspires beauty. There is nothing in the world as beautiful as the Eucharist. The art that Christ inspires is enduring.

೭ುಲ

Parishes mark the feast of Corpus Christi in countless ways. Some schedule extended periods of adoration, when the Host consecrated during Mass is exposed on the altar, in a ciborium or a monstrance.

Some churches sponsor processions. A Corpus Christi procession, according to the documents of the Church, "is a prolongation of the celebration of the Eucharist: immediately after Mass, the Sacred Host, consecrated during the Mass, is borne out of the Church for the Christian faithful 'to make public profession of faith and worship of the Most Blessed Sacrament.'"[1] In these processions, God's people are journeying with the Lord and proclaiming faith in Emmanuel, Jesus Christ, who is truly God with us (see Matthew 1:23).

At the end of Saint Matthew's Gospel, Jesus makes the Church a solemn promise: "I am with you always" (Matthew 28:20); and through the Eucharist, he is truly present to us. But the story does not end there. The Lord we receive in the Mass is also present in our tabernacles. He is present in our monstrances and our processions, when we take him out into the world to proclaim him publicly as our King and Lord.

---

1 Congregation for Divine Worship, *Directory on Popular Piety and the Liturgy*, 162.

Children celebrating Corpus Christi in the year of their first Communion.

Corpus Christi is a powerful sign, but like every sign it points to something still greater. The truth is that we take Christ into the world whenever we receive Holy Communion. We have received Christ and become one with him. We are his face and voice and hands and feet in the world.

After *every* Mass our walk of faith, our eucharistic procession, continues. Like the first disciples, we are called to walk with Jesus, to be his witnesses as we live our faith by loving and serving others. Every day we can join a "Corpus Christi procession"—a procession of the Body and Blood of Christ—in our homes, schools, workplaces, and communities.

CHAPTER 13

The Solemnity of Christ the King and Other Feasts of Jesus

"The kingdom of the world has become the kingdom of our Lord and of his Christ, and he shall reign for ever and ever."
—Revelation 11:15

As November draws to a close, bumper stickers and window signs remind us that "Jesus is the reason for the season." The slogan is meant for Christmas, of course, but it applies equally to every season and every feast. The Church is always celebrating Jesus Christ in his paschal mystery, even when Easter is months away.

The last Sunday of the Church year is dedicated to Jesus in a special way. It is the Solemnity of Christ the King. The Church's new year begins with the First Sunday of Advent, and this feast falls on the last Sunday in the season of Ordinary Time, late in November. Like Easter, it is a moveable feast—that is, a feast with a variable date—but it always falls on a Sunday.

The Solemnity of Christ the King is a relative newcomer to the Church calendar. It was added in 1925 by Pope Pius XI. In 1969 Pope Paul VI gave the feast a fuller title: Our Lord Jesus Christ, King of the Universe.

The feasts are never didactic or preachy, but they always have a point to make. *Lex orandi, lex credendi,* runs an old Latin saying, which roughly translates as: *The law of prayer is the law of belief.* As we live the feasts, so we live the faith. In establishing a feast in honor of Jesus's Kingship, Pope Pius XI was forthright about the doctrinal point he was trying to make. He intended the new feast to be an antidote to the poison of secularism, which was then spreading in deadly forms throughout the world.

In Mexico in the mid-1920s, anti-Catholic laws made the practice of the faith a capital crime, and thousands of men, women, and children were martyred. In the lands dominated since 1917 by the communist USSR, belief in God was effectively illegal. Elsewhere in Europe, many traditionally Christian lands were turning to forms of government that placed the concerns of the state above everything else, including matters of conscience and religion. Violence against the clergy and the vandalism of churches were on the rise. Meanwhile, citizens in some affluent democracies were simply losing interest in religion and giving over their lives to the pursuit of pleasure.

Pope Pius instituted the feast of Christ the King with his encyclical *Quas Primas,* which still serves as a radical Christian critique of the many forms of godlessness in modern society. He predicted that dire consequences were looming for all people. " 'With God and Jesus Christ excluded from political life, with authority derived not from God but from man, the very basis of that authority has been taken away. . . . The result is that human society is tottering to its fall, because it has no longer a secure and solid foundation.'"[1]

Within two decades of his warning, the foundations did indeed begin to crumble.

The world's economy became mired in a Great Depression, brought on by greed and excess consumption. Nations rose against one another in World War II. Dictators condemned millions to death through racist and genocidal laws. The first atomic bombs fell to earth, vaporizing thousands of lives in an instant.

In hindsight, Pius XI seems ominously prophetic. Yet his encyclical was not intended to be a herald of doom and gloom. He wrote it to establish a great *feast*—a day of celebration—for the whole world. He wanted to proclaim Christ's reign over everyone and everything, "collectively or individually," "the individual and the family or the State." All are already "under the dominion of Christ."[2]

Jesus's jurisdiction is universal. He reigns over the natural and supernatural order. He leaves people free to accept or reject his law. But the law remains a law, and those who break it bring on inexorable consequences. When rulers and peoples throw off the gentle yoke of Christ, they inevitably choose disaster.

Yet Pius remained hopeful. "When once men recognize, both in private and in public life, that Christ is King, society will at last receive the great blessings of real liberty, well-ordered discipline, peace and harmony."[3]

---

1 Pope Pius XI, *Quas Primas* (encyclical on the Feast of Christ the King), December 11, 1925, 18.

2 Ibid.

3 Ibid., 19.

Almost all of the empires and governments that worried Pius XI have vanished from the earth, but the Church still calls us to proclaim Christ as King. In our time, secularists in our "developed" Western nations treat the name of Christ as an expletive to be deleted from all public discourse. They have ordained that religion is the only topic that may never be discussed in polite company. Now as in ancient times, "The kings of the earth set themselves, and the rulers take counsel together, against the Lord and his anointed" (Psalm 2:2).

Even in such times the Church rejoices, because the victory is assured: "they will make war on the Lamb," but "the Lamb will conquer them, for he is Lord of lords and King of kings" (Revelation 17:14).

Christ conquers not by violence but by persevering love. He reigns over this world, but his "kingship is not of this world" (John 18:36). So the Solemnity of Christ the King, arriving as it does at the end of the year, turns the Church's attention to "last things." As Christians we persistently pray, "Thy kingdom come," and we see our prayer answered every day in beautiful ways, some small and some great. One day that prayer will be fulfilled in perfect glory, when Christ comes as triumphant King.

ॐ

Jesus Christ is the object of every action of the Church. He is implicitly the focus of every feast day. Even in the feasts of the saints, he is glorified because he is their life. But certain feasts draw our attention to particular characteristics of Jesus or events in his own earthly life.

Christians in many places celebrate the feasts of Our Lord by processions through the streets of their towns and cities.

The Solemnity of the Sacred Heart of Jesus, a moveable feast, falls on the Friday following the second Sunday after Pentecost. The term "Sacred Heart" stands for the entire mystery of Jesus Christ, "the totality of his being . . . Son of God, uncreated wisdom; infinite charity, principal of the salvation and sanctification of mankind."[4] Jesus's heart figures prominently in the story of salvation. He revealed himself as "gentle and lowly in heart" (Matthew 11:29). Upon his death, his side was pierced with a lance, and blood and water flowed from the wound (John 19:34); Christians have always seen this as symbolic of the sacraments of salvation—baptism and the Eucharist. After he rose from the dead, Jesus invited the apostle Thomas to put his hand into his side (John 20:27). These events influenced the development of the Church's devotion to the Sacred Heart, a devotion that emphasizes his charity and tender mercy. In the seventeenth century, when the heresy of Jansenism emphasized the rigors of divine justice, devotion to the Sacred Heart flourished and served as an antidote, inspiring the faithful to trust in Jesus's mercy. It was then that the feast was established in the universal Church; the devotion is quite ancient, and traces can be found in the early Church Fathers.

The Solemnity of the Annunciation of the Lord, March 25, commemorates the conception of Jesus, by the power of the Holy Spirit, in the womb of the Virgin Mary. For many of the early Christians, the Annunciation

---

4 Congregation for Divine Worship, *Directory on Popular Piety and the Liturgy*, 166.

was the great feast of the incarnation, because it marked the very moment when the Word became flesh, when God's human life began. Since the era of grace began on that very day, some secular governments also marked it as the beginning of the New Year. The message of the annunciation is implicitly pro-life: Jesus's human life began at his conception. For this reason, among many others, the early Christians condemned abortion in the strongest terms. In the twentieth century, as technology presented many new threats to the unborn, Catholics have increasingly observed the Annunciation as a pro-life feast day and a day of special prayer for society's most vulnerable.

The Feast of the Presentation of the Lord, February 2, celebrates the incident described in the second chapter of Luke's Gospel (2:22–40). Jesus's parents, Mary and Joseph, go to Jerusalem to fulfill the ritual laws required of Jews after the birth of a child. According to the Law, Jesus, as a firstborn son, had to be "ransomed" or "redeemed" by his parents. Mary would need to undergo the rites for purification after childbirth. Of course, as Redeemer, Jesus needed no redemption; nor did sinless Mary need to be purified. But in obedience and humility the Holy Family submitted to the Law. The feast day celebrates the joyful encounter between the Messiah and his people, represented by Simeon and Anna, an elderly man and woman who prophesy regarding the child's life and mission. The feast is sometimes called Candlemas, because candles are blessed on that day, or the Feast of the Purification of the Blessed Virgin Mary.

Mosaic of the presentation of the baby Jesus in the Temple.

The Feast of the Transfiguration of the Lord, August 6, recalls the day when Jesus appeared in glorious form to his apostles Peter, James, and John. They had gone to a high mountain to pray, and there Jesus's appearance became dazzling. He was joined by the Old Testament lawgiver Moses and the prophet Elijah. The episode appears in three of the Gospels (Matthew 17:1-9, Mark 9:2-9, Luke 9:28-36) and is mentioned in one of the New Testament letters (2 Peter 1:16-18). The Church has always considered the transfiguration to be a special revelation of the Blessed Trinity, since the Father appears in a voice from above, Jesus is there as the Son, and the Holy Spirit appears as the cloud of glory. The feast was celebrated in the first millennium and was made universal in the fifteenth century.

The Memorial of the Holy Name of Jesus, January 13, pays homage to the name that heaven chose for the Savior. It is an optional memorial. Both Mary (Luke 1:31) and Joseph (Matthew 1:21) learned from angels the name they were to give their Son. He would be called Jesus, "for he will save his people from their sins" (Matthew 1:21). In Hebrew, the name means "God saves." Since the time of the apostles, the Church has honored Jesus's name in a special way. Saint Paul said: "at the name of Jesus every knee should bow, in heaven and on earth and under the earth" (Philippians 2:10). Jesus's name itself has saving power: "every one who calls upon the name of the Lord will be saved" (Romans 10:13).

CHAPTER 14

The Solemnity of the Most Holy Trinity

The grace of the Lord Jesus Christ and the love of God and
the fellowship of the Holy Spirit be with you all.
—2 Corinthians 13:14

THE SOLEMNITY OF THE MOST Holy Trinity honors not an event but a truth revealed by Jesus Christ—and according to the Catholic faith, it is the most important truth of all. Trinity Sunday celebrates the eternal life of God, who is one and yet is three divine persons: the Father, the Son, and the Holy Spirit. Trinity Sunday is celebrated on the Sunday after Pentecost.

From the beginning, the Church has worshiped God as a Trinity of divine persons in undivided unity. So many of the early prayers, and especially the liturgies of the ancient Church, include repeated doxologies of the Trinity. Catholic prayer still keeps this focus, and the Church teaches that "every genuine form of popular piety" is trinitarian and "must necessarily refer to God, 'the all-powerful Father, His only begotten Son and the Holy Spirit.'"[1]

---

1 Congregation for Divine Worship, *Directory on Popular Piety and the Liturgy*, 157.

When we make the sign of the cross, we pray "in the name of the Father, and of the Son, and of the Holy Spirit." When we baptize, we do so with the same trinitarian formula, "thereby beginning a life of intimacy with the God, as sons of the Father, brothers of Jesus, and temples of the Holy Spirit."[2] Two of our most commonly used prayers are the "little doxology" (*Glory be to the Father, and to the Son, and to the Holy Spirit . . .*) and the "great doxology" (*Glory to God in the highest . . .*). "Worship," the Church tells us, is inherently trinitarian. It is "the dialogue of God with man through Christ in the Holy Spirit."[3]

The *Catechism of the Catholic Church* makes the matter abundantly clear.

> The mystery of the Most Holy Trinity is the central mystery of Christian faith and life. It is the mystery of God in himself. It is therefore the source of all the other mysteries of faith, the light that enlightens them. It is the most fundamental and essential teaching in the "hierarchy of the truths of faith." (CCC, 234)

It seems so natural to celebrate the Trinity that many centuries ago some theologians argued that a feast would be redundant. Every Sunday, they said, was "Trinity Sunday"—because the Mass is fundamentally a trinitarian prayer. Yet many local churches went ahead anyway and celebrated a day in honor of the triune God. After all, a similar argument could be employed against Easter ("Every Sunday celebrates the resurrection"). In

2 Ibid.
3 Ibid., 158.

The three divine persons of the Trinity are manifest
at Jesus's baptism: the voice of the Father, the person
of the Son, and the dove of the Spirit.

1334 Pope John XXII established Trinity Sunday as a feast for the entire Latin Church.

The truth about the Trinity is so mysterious that it exceeds human understanding. It is inaccessible to unaided reason. No team of researchers could have fathomed the mystery, even after a long lifetime of exploration. The Church teaches that reason alone can indeed conclude that God *exists,* but reason by itself could never know *that God is a Trinity of persons.*

It is through the incarnation that God revealed himself to be an eternal communion of persons—a family. In a now famous homily preached early in his pontificate, Pope Saint John Paul II said: "God in His deepest mystery is not a solitude, but a family, since he has in himself fatherhood, sonship and the essence of the family, which is love."[4]

God the Father revealed the Trinity by sending the Son into the world to bestow the Spirit. So God's self-revelation in Jesus Christ, the Eternal Word, is not simply a disclosure of information. It is a sharing of life. It is the essence of our salvation.

The readings for Trinity Sunday show how the revelation of the Trinity was prefigured in the Old Testament and then fully disclosed in Jesus's life. But even in the New Testament this revelation is like a light that is so bright it left the apostles stunned. In the epistles, Saint Paul struggled to express the mystery that he knows to be true.

The Trinity is the deepest mystery, and it is the truth at the foundation of all other truth. If we say that "God is love" (1 John 4:16), we can do so only because we know that God is

---

4 Pope Saint John Paul II, homily at Palafox Major Seminary, Puebla de Los Angeles, Mexico, January 28, 1979.

not a solitude, but a communion, a plurality. God is a lover from all eternity because he has a coeternal object of his love.

This is not a truth we can adequately explain or work out mathematically. Yet the Church is utterly dependent upon it, and everything we believe about other loves—the loves we call "charity" and "marriage"—is utterly dependent upon the eternal love we know in the Trinity.

At baptism we come to share the life of Jesus Christ. Living in God's eternal Son, we too become his children, and we share the life of the Blessed Trinity. That is the very definition of heaven, but we begin to experience it now on earth. The early Christians celebrated that fact and called it not only our "salvation," but our "divinization" and "deification." By grace, Christians become godlike—we become gods (see John 10:34). God shares his divine life with us and makes us like himself (2 Peter 1:4, Galatians 2:20).

The Church Fathers clung tenaciously to the doctrine of the Trinity and guarded it jealously. They were willing to be exiled and even to die defending the Church's creeds. Their passion rings clear to us even after nearly two thousand years. Saint Gregory Nazianzen preached in the fourth century:

Above all guard for me this great deposit of faith for which I live and fight, which I want to take with me as a companion, and which makes me bear all evils and despise all pleasures: I mean the profession of faith in the Father and the Son and the Holy Spirit. I entrust it to you today. By it I am soon going to plunge you into water and raise you up from it. I give it to you as the companion and patron of your whole life. I give you but one divinity and power, existing one in three, and containing the three in a distinct way.

Divinity without disparity of substance or nature, without superior degree that raises up or inferior degree that casts down . . . the infinite co-naturality of three infinites. Each person considered in himself is entirely God . . . the three considered together. . . . I have not even begun to think of unity when the Trinity bathes me in its splendor. I have not even begun to think of the Trinity when unity grasps me.[5]

The Trinity is the truth at the foundation of all other truth. Whole volumes and libraries could not contain its riches. Nor can a feast once a year. But that is, itself, a reason to celebrate.

---

5 St. Gregory of Nazianzus, *Oratio* 40, 41:PG 36, 417, quoted in CCC, 256.

CHAPTER 15

The Solemnity of Divine Mercy

O give thanks to the Lord, for he is good,
for his steadfast love endures for ever.
—Psalm 136:1

DIVINE MERCY SUNDAY IS THE newest major addition to the Church's calendar. Established in the year 2000 by Pope Saint John Paul II, it arrived on a wave of devotion to God's mercy that had been swelling in the Church since the middle of the last century.

The Church is both a mother and a teacher, and the feasts are always timely lessons she delivers to her children—giving us something we otherwise lack, or fortifying us against some emerging challenge. We have seen that in our studies of the feasts of Epiphany, Corpus Christi, and Christ the King. Those feasts are perennial gifts to the Church, but each arose to address an urgent need.

If Divine Mercy is the feast for our moment in history, then it certainly contains a lesson for our time. As we examine the feasts in general, we must pay special attention to this one in particular. If we believe that the Church is guided by the Holy Spirit, then it is good for us to ask why this feast has appeared at this time.

Divine Mercy is a solemnity celebrated on the Sunday after Easter—the final day of the Easter Octave. Pope John Paul discovered the devotion through the diaries kept by a visionary nun whose life overlapped with his own. Sister Faustina Kowalska spent all her brief life (1905–1938) in Poland and Lithuania. She had only a rudimentary education, and she occupied humble positions, cooking and cleaning in convents.

From her late-teen years, she experienced apparitions of Jesus, who taught her a profound theology of his mercy. She recorded his teaching in her diaries, which filled several volumes. Though she met with opposition, disbelief, and disinterest, she strove to carry out the mission Jesus entrusted to her: to promote devotion to his merciful love. He asked her to commission the painting of an image depicting him just as she saw him, with penetrating rays of mercy emanating from his heart. She carefully recorded his instruction: "I want the image to be solemnly blessed on the first Sunday after Easter, and I want it to be venerated publicly so that every soul may know about it."[1]

Faustina also reported the form that devotion to Divine Mercy should take. The Divine Mercy Chaplet, which she promoted, includes traditional prayers—such as the Lord's Prayer, the Hail Mary, and the Trisagion (the "Thrice Holy" hymn)—"Holy God, Holy Mighty One, Holy Immortal One, have mercy on us"—supplemented by new prayers revealed in Sister Faustina's visions.

---

1 Saint Faustina Kowalska, *Diary: Divine Mercy in My Soul* (Stockbridge, Mass.: Marians of the Immaculate Conception, 2002), 341.

Among the extraordinary graces she received was fore-knowledge of World War II, which was about to erupt in Europe, beginning with the invasion of her own homeland. Divine Mercy devotion was perhaps God's way of preparing the world for the healing to follow. Sister Faustina died a year before the war began. The devotion spread, however, during the difficult years that followed—years of Nazi occupation in Eastern Europe, followed by Soviet oppression. Around this time, Poland became the epicenter of a new and powerful movement in Catholic spirituality.

Saint John Paul II, the Polish pope, elected in 1978, brought Divine Mercy devotion to the attention of the whole Church. Even Catholics who shy away from apparitions and extraordinary phenomena became aware of it. The devotions became a fixture in parishes—and even on television. Faustina was canonized a saint in the Jubilee Year 2000, and at the same time John Paul instituted the Solemnity of Divine Mercy.

The devotion drew upon images that were already associated with the Second Sunday of Easter. The Gospel of the day tells the story of Jesus's invitation to Thomas to touch his wounds. In Faustina's visions, and in the Divine Mercy image she commissioned, Jesus appears with mercy shining forth from his wounded side.

Saint Faustina Kowalska saw coming from this Heart that was overflowing with generous love, two rays of light which illuminated the world. "The two rays," according to what Jesus himself told her, "represent the blood and the water" (Diary, p. 132). The blood recalls the sacrifice of Golgotha and the mystery of the Eucharist; the water, according to the rich symbolism of the Evangelist John, makes us think of Baptism and the Gift of the Holy Spirit (cf. Jn 3:5; 4:14).

Through the mystery of this wounded heart, the restorative tide of God's merciful love continues to spread over the men and women of our time. Here alone can those who long for true and lasting happiness find its secret.[2]

The theme of divine mercy has continued—and, in fact, grown stronger—in the years since Saint John Paul's passing. Pope Francis has even been called "the Pope of Mercy." He has called the present time "a time of mercy" and a "*kairos* of mercy," using the Greek word for "a moment appointed by God." Francis took as his papal motto *Miserando atque eligendo*—"by mercy and by choosing." Soon after his election, the pope remarked that it was time for the Church to heal wounds. When a reporter asked him how the Church would do that, he replied: "With mercy."

Mercy is the special "necessity" of the Church in our time, said Pope Francis. It is arguable that mercy is always in season. Still, the Church speaks through her feasts, and the establishment of this particular feast is a grace that begins providentially with this millennial generation. "He who has an ear, let him hear what the Spirit says to the churches" (Revelation 2:7).

---

2 Pope Saint John Paul II, Homily for Divine Mercy Sunday, April 22, 2001.

CHAPTER 16

Feasts of the Blessed Virgin Mary

For behold, henceforth all generations
will call me blessed;
for he who is mighty has done great things
for me, and holy is his name.
—Luke 1:48-49

THE BLESSED VIRGIN MARY IS a beautiful, beloved, essential, and pervasive figure in the Christian calendar, and she has been since the early days of the Church. If we compiled a calendar of only her feasts, memorials, and solemnities, it would be fairly full, and it could justify a book all on its own. Each of her feasts has special traditions, customs, and habits of piety, and they are as varied as the cultures of the world.

All the Marian feasts are feasts of Jesus Christ, for she has no privilege that she has not received from God. Her "soul magnifies the Lord" (Luke 1:46), and to celebrate her is to celebrate God's greatest creation—the vessel he fashioned to be his own mother, the woman who would bear him into the world.

All the Marian feasts are feasts of Jesus Christ—but she is

near in all the feasts of Jesus as well, because she is always near her son. To celebrate Christmas, we draw "round yon Virgin Mother and Child." On Good Friday, as we recall Jesus's Passion, she is "at the cross, her station keeping." The Gospels show her near her son from the moment of his conception through his childhood and adolescence. When the magi go looking for the newborn King, they find him in the arms of his mother. She is there, too, at the beginning of his public ministry (John 2:1), and it is her intercession that moves Jesus to begin his mission prematurely, by his own account. But he had always been obedient to her (Luke 2:51). That was the choice of omniscient wisdom.

Mary followed Jesus through his years of preaching (see Matthew 12:46), and she was one of the very few disciples who stayed with him as he was dying on the cross (John 19:25–27).

So the Church cannot help but think often of Jesus's mother. In doing so, we imitate the Lord himself. Like the Gospels, the calendar provides the Church with moments in the close company of the Mother of Jesus. We who are saved are now members of the Holy Family, along with Mary and Joseph. Since Jesus is our brother, his Father is "Our Father"; his home is our home; and his mother is our mother. The Church delights in that fact and celebrates it with many special days.

The Church honors her every Saturday, recalling the one full day that Jesus spent in the tomb. According to tradition, Mary was the disciple who best kept the faith on that day. The early Church took up the practice of keeping faith with her on that day each week. The early Church in Rome kept the Saturday before Pentecost as a special feast of Our Lady, because of her presence with the apostles as they awaited the coming of the Holy Spirit (see Acts 1:14).

Since the Middle Ages the Church has devoted the month of May to Mary, and many Christians undertake pilgrimages during that month to shrines associated with the Blessed Virgin. Many parishes have "May Crownings," in which a statue of the Blessed Mother is adorned with a diadem or a wreath of flowers. The month of October, too, has long been associated with the Rosary, the Church's most popular Marian devotion.

The Church's attention to Mary—love for Mary—is based on her relationship to Jesus Christ. Her son is God's Eternal Word who came to dwell among us. Mary's son came to reveal to us who God is, to teach us the meaning of life, and to help us live. This could not have happened without Mary and her "yes" to God. As a mother, Mary brought Christ to the world. We do not worship her as God, but we honor her uniquely as *Mother of God,* because Jesus is God, and she mothered him throughout his earthly sojourn. A mother never ceases to be a mother.

With his last breaths, Jesus gave her to all Christians. From the cross he looked at the disciple whom he loved and said: "Behold, your mother!" (John 19:27). And that disciple, Saint John, took her into his home, but he did it as the Church's representative—as the representative of *every* beloved disciple. As our spiritual mother, Mary still leads us to Jesus. She says: "Do whatever he tells you" (John 2:5). And she helps us as we lead others to know and love her Son. Her feasts empower us to do this with greater love.

The Solemnity of Mary, Mother of God, January 1, is a very ancient feast. The fifth-century Council of Ephesus, which affirmed Jesus's true divinity and true humanity, also declared Mary to be Theotokos, God-bearer. As Mary is the Mother of Jesus, so she is the

Mother of God. There can be no greater honor for a human being.

The Solemnity of the Assumption of the Blessed Virgin Mary, August 15, commemorates the fact that Mary was taken into heaven ("assumed"), body and soul, at the end of her earthly days. It is an ancient feast. In the East, it is traditionally called Mary's Dormition, her "falling asleep."

The Solemnity of the Immaculate Conception of the Blessed Virgin Mary, December 8, celebrates Mary's sinlessness from the moment she was conceived in the womb. By the power of Jesus's redemption, she was preserved from any stain of original sin or personal sin. She received this grace in virtue of the merits of Jesus Christ.

The Feast of the Visitation of the Blessed Virgin Mary, May 31, marks Mary's journey to care for her kinswoman Elizabeth, the mother of Saint John the Baptist. The arrival of the Messiah is first publicly revealed to the people of Israel, appearing to poor shepherds in Bethlehem.

The Feast of the Birth of the Blessed Virgin Mary, September 8, is a very unusual observance. Most saints are honored for the day they entered heaven. Since Mary was always sinless, she is honored even for her birth and conception (and these feasts are exactly nine months apart).

Memorial of the Immaculate Heart of Mary, a moveable feast, falls on the Saturday following the second Sunday after Pentecost. It honors the inner life of Mary, her joys and sorrows (see Luke 2:19, 35, 51).

The Memorial of the Queenship of Blessed Virgin Mary, August 22, recognizes the special role that God has given Mary in the ongoing history of salvation. Revelation 12:1 shows the Mother of the Messiah in heaven, with a crown of twelve stars.

The Optional Memorial of the Most Holy Name of the Blessed Virgin Mary, September 12, was added to the calendar to commemorate the victory of Christian forces at the Battle of Vienna in 1683. The victory was decisive in turning back Islamic forces then advancing on Europe; Christian leaders attributed their success to Mary's intercession. Devotion to Mary's name is very ancient.

The Memorial of the Presentation of the Blessed Virgin Mary, November 21, marks the day when Mary's parents presented her in the Temple and dedicated her life to God.

The Optional Memorial of Our Lady of Lourdes, February 11, commemorates Mary's appearance to a young girl, Bernadette Soubirous, in 1858. Many sick people have been healed on pilgrimage to the site of the apparition in Lourdes, France. The Church also observes the date as World Day of Prayer for the Sick.

The Optional Memorial of Our Lady of Fátima, May 13, recalls the appearance of the Blessed Virgin to three young children in Portugal in 1917. The messages of Mary at Fatima have been very influential in the Church's life, and many believe they foretold significant events, such as the rise and fall of communism, and the assassination attempt on Pope Saint John Paul II.

The Optional Memorial of Our Lady of Mount Carmel, July 16, marks the date when, according to tradition, Mary appeared to Saint Simon Stock, a Carmelite friar, and initiated the practice of wearing the brown scapular. The scapular of Our Lady of Mount Carmel is "an external sign of the filial relationship established between the Blessed Virgin Mary, Mother and Queen of Mount Carmel, and the faithful who entrust themselves totally to her protection, who have recourse to her maternal intercession, who are mindful of the primacy of the spiritual life and the need for prayer."[1]

The Memorial of Our Lady of Sorrows, September 15, recalls the sufferings endured by Mary in her earthly life, foretold in Simeon's prophecy (Luke 2:34-35). The prophecy itself is the first sorrow; the others are the flight into Egypt, the loss of the child Jesus in the Temple, the meeting of Mary and Jesus on the way to Calvary, the crucifixion, the taking down of Jesus from the cross, and his burial.

---

1 Congregation for Divine Worship, *Directory on Popular Piety and the Liturgy,* 205.

Memorial of Our Lady of the Rosary, October 7, formerly known as the Feast of Our Lady of Victory, honors Mary for her intercessory power. The feast was established by Pope Pius V in thanksgiving for the victory of Christian forces at the Battle of Lepanto, after the pope had called on all Christians in Europe to pray the Rosary.

Feast of Our Lady of Guadalupe, December 12, commemorates Mary's appearance in 1531 to Juan Diego, a poor native Mexican. She appeared as a pregnant native woman and spoke his language, relating to him through her humility and poverty. The incident led to mass conversions on the American continents. In 1945 Pope Pius XII designated Our Lady of Guadalupe as patroness of the Americas.

On Marian feasts the faithful make pilgrimages to
shrines of the Blessed Virgin.

CHAPTER 17

The Solemnity of All Saints—and Other Saints and Souls

> *But you have come to Mount Zion and to the city of the living God, the heavenly Jerusalem, and to innumerable angels in festal gathering, and to the assembly of the first-born who are enrolled in heaven.*
> —Hebrews 12:22-23

"YOU HAVE MADE US FOR YOURSELF, O Lord, and our hearts are restless until they rest in you," Saint Augustine wrote in his *Confessions.*

Centuries earlier, at the dawn of Christianity, Saint Irenaeus said, "The glory of God is man fully alive, and the life of man is the vision of God."[1]

To rest in God, to be fully alive, to see God—these, for the Church, are synonymous terms. They describe the basic qualities of Christian life. They describe the life of the saints.

---

1 Saint Irenaeus of Lyons, *Against Heresies* 4.20.7.

In this mural, an array of notable American Catholics—laity, clergy, and
religious—represent the universality of the call to holiness.

When most people think of saints they think of plaster stat-
ues standing in churches. They think of holy cards. They think
of famous names whose feasts have become fixtures even in the
secular calendar—Saint Patrick, for example, on March 17, and
Saint Valentine on February 14. There are thousands of these
official, "canonized" saints, and hundreds of their names appear
on the calendar, with memorials or optional memorials. These
are people who by their heroic virtue have demonstrated a particular closeness to Christ and have offered witness to the rest
of the Church of what it means to follow in the footsteps of the
Lord. Their feast days are our annual reminders of their great
example and their intercessory power before the throne of God.

Some saints are universally acclaimed such as Saint Francis
of Assisi and Saint Thérèse of Lisieux. Others are better known

and appreciated within their own local or religious communities. The Capuchin Franciscans, for example, keep a lively devotion to the canonized and beatified members of their order. The people of Baltimore, Chicago, and Pittsburgh remember in a special way the saints who have lived in their cities.

As part of Catholic devotion we speak of invoking or "praying to" the saints, "on whose constant intercession we rely for help" (Eucharistic Prayer III). We do not address the saints in the same way we call upon God. To invoke the intercession of the saints, including Mary, is really to pray that, together with them, we may grow in the love of the triune God who wills the salvation of all. We ask for their prayers the way we would ask the prayers of anyone else in our family. We express the longing that the saints' living and personal love of God will also embrace us and that by their prayers we can be assisted in obtaining benefits from God.

We know of the saints' intercessory power through the witness of Holy Scripture. Saint John saw, in heaven, four living creatures (angels) with "golden bowls full of incense, which are the prayers of the saints" (Revelation 5:8). The letter to the Hebrews tells us that the saints in glory take a lively interest in our lives on earth; they surround us as a great "cloud of witnesses" (Hebrews 12:1).

Through the Church's tradition we know of thousands of saints who are in heaven. Yet we know, too, that there are many others—perhaps many millions—whose goodness and holiness are remembered only in heaven. Many good and holy people have lived and died and never been officially recognized by the Church—at least not through the canonization process. Now their lives are "hid with Christ in God" (Colossians 3:3)—but they are truly at rest and fully alive because they behold the vision of God.

They are saints because *only* saints are in heaven, and we must become saints if we are to enter heaven. Saint Paul uses the Greek word for "saint" (*hagios*) to describe living Christians as well as the faithful departed (see Romans 15:25-26, Colossians 1:12). In its most basic sense, "sainthood"—sanctity, holiness—is the condition of someone who is baptized. Every Christian has received holiness as a grace from God, who alone is truly holy. We must, however, live up to the gift. We must freely accept it and apply it faithfully in our day-to-day lives.

Not all the saints are famous, but all of them get their day on the calendar, because the Church celebrates the Solemnity of All Saints on November 1 in the Latin Church. It is a holy day of obligation. In the first half of the first millennium, many local churches kept a date to commemorate all the martyrs—or at least all the local martyrs. Gradually, the feasts coalesced in a single day for the whole Church and all the saints, martyrs and non-martyrs, known and unknown.

When Christians recite the Apostles Creed, we profess our belief in "the communion of saints." We believe that we share a close family bond with all the "holy ones"—those who are living among us and those who have ended their earthly days. We count them all in the communion. For those who have died, life has changed, not ended, because the soul is immortal. There is one Church, and it encompasses those who are already in heaven as well as those on their way to heaven. All Christians live together "in Christ."

It is customary in some places for children to dress up as their favorite saints on the eve of the feast day—formerly called the Eve of All Hallows, or Hallow E'en. Children still dress up on Halloween, and it is an admirable custom to put on the appearance of the men, women, and angels they admire.

༂

The day after All Saints' Day is All Souls' Day—officially, the Commemoration of All Faithful Departed.

We believe the soul is immortal. It does not die. At the end of their earthly days, all souls go to judgment, and they proceed to the destiny they have chosen based on the way they lived their lives on earth. The just go to God; and the unjust continue on the path they have chosen, away from God, away from glory, away from heaven.

Even the just sin during their time on earth (see Proverbs 24:16). "All have sinned and fall short of the glory of God" (Romans 3:23). Yet "nothing unclean shall enter" heaven (Revelation 21:27). Thus Christians since ancient times have believed that souls destined for heaven first undergo a period of purification. In the tradition of the Latin Church this condition or place is called *purgatory*.

Jews in the time of Jesus kept the custom of praying for the dead. We see it in the Second Book of Maccabees when the leader of the Jewish army arranges sacrifices for the sake of those who had died in battle. The sacred author tells us that it is "a holy and pious thought," to make "atonement for the dead, that they might be delivered from their sin" (2 Maccabees 12:45-46). We find the same principle at work in the New Testament when Saint Paul offers atonement on behalf of others: "in my flesh I complete what is lacking in Christ's afflictions for the sake of his body, that is, the church" (Colossians 1:24).

Those who have died are still members of the Church, and the Church cherishes their memory, especially on All Souls' Day every year. A significant part of this tradition is the practice of having a Mass celebrated for the repose of the soul of a beloved deceased person. In this holy remembrance we both pray for the dead and affirm our solidarity with them in Christ through the Eucharist.

It is customary in many places to visit the graves of deceased family members on this day and to pray for the repose of their soul. This, too, is "a holy and pious thought."

Though the Church usually discourages priests from celebrating Mass more than twice in a day, they are permitted on All Souls' Day to celebrate three Masses for the dead.

෨ඏ

It is natural for us to remember heroes. We build civic monuments to past presidents, and we even observe their birthdays as federal holidays. When we do this we are following the example of the early Christians.

It was common practice in the early Church to record the names of the martyrs and the dates of their death. Christians would also step forward to collect the martyrs' bodies—or what was left of them—after the execution of their sentence. In cases where they were burned at the stake or torn apart by lions, the collection could be quite difficult.

The faithful lovingly kept those relics and built monuments to the martyrs. Every year they would observe the date of each martyr's passing as his or her *dies natalis*—literally, "birthday," because it was on that day that the martyr was born to eternal life. Many of the oldest churches in the city of Rome were built over the sites where the martyrs had been buried.

The Church kept the saints' "birthdays" by worshiping God, offering the sacrifice of the Mass, and celebrating a feast. In the Eucharist the Church gives thanks to God for the lives of the saints—the difference they made in their years on earth, the difference they continue to make through their intercession in heaven.

The ancient feast of the apostles Peter and Paul, on June 29, is now kept as a solemnity, and in many places it is a holy day of obligation. The Church also observes a Feast of the Conversion of Saint Paul, January 25, and a Feast of the Chair of Saint Peter, February 22.

Most saints are remembered with simple memorials—like Saint Francis of Assisi on October 4 and Saint Thérèse of Lisieux on October 1. Other saints are so universally and ardently loved, and have been since ancient times, that their days are kept as feasts for the entire Church. All of the apostles' "birthdays" are kept as feasts; but so is the *dies natalis* of the third-century deacon Saint Lawrence of Rome, who was known for his charity and his sense of humor.

One of the great joys of living in a family is gathering for birthdays and anniversaries. It's only natural to look forward to such reunions. Grace builds on nature, and so our sacred memorials are all the more festive. They involve a bigger family.

We should not forget our loved ones who have passed on. The great ones in the Church we remember as saints, and we hold them close. The familiar ones we lived with, in our homes and neighborhoods, we recall as well, and we pray for their repose, and it is a holy and wholesome thought when we do.

As we celebrate the feasts of the saints, we pass on to the next generation the memories we have received from our ancestors. We give the children of the next generation their models for fidelity, for happy marriage, for courage, for perseverance, for charity, and for joy.

CHAPTER 18

The Holy Angels

For he will give his angels charge of you
to guard you in all your ways.
—Psalm 91:11

Bless the Lord, O you his angels,
you mighty ones who do his word,
hearkening to the voice of his word!
—Psalm 103:20

WE KNOW FROM THE SCRIPTURES that humankind makes up just a small portion of the spiritual beings in creation. Human beings are composed of spirit and matter, body and soul, but the Bible tells us that God created many *pure* spirits as well. We tend to call them all "angels," colloquially, though the Scriptures speak of different types or orders—seraphim, cherubim, thrones, dominions, virtues, powers, principalities, angels, and archangels. The sacred authors mention the names of only three angels. The Church celebrates them on the Feast

Saint Michael the Archangel, defender of the Church.

of Saints Michael, Gabriel, and Raphael, on September 29. It is also called "The Feast of Saint Michael and All Angels" or sometimes Michaelmas. A few days later, on October 2, comes the Memorial of the Guardian Angels.

Anyone who reads the Bible attentively knows that angels have played pivotal roles in human history. It was an angel who held back the hand of Abraham when he was ready to sacrifice Isaac, his son. Moses received the law through the ministry of angels. The prophets, too, received their oracles from the heavenly messengers. Angels announced the conception of Jesus to Mary and Joseph—and heralded his birth to the shepherds. Angels ministered to Jesus as he fasted in the desert, and they attended him again when he suffered in the Garden of Gethsemane. Angels stood by Jesus's tomb on the day he rose from the dead, and they bore witness to his ascension into heaven. Angels guided the ministry of the apostles and the newborn Church; an angel helped Saint Peter to escape from prison. And angels appeared in multitudes in the book of Revelation, continuing to guide the course of earthly events.

Angels (contrary to popular misconception) are not disembodied human souls. We don't become angels when we die. According to the *Catechism,* an angel is a spiritual, personal, and immortal creature, with intelligence and free will, who glorifies God ceaselessly and who serves God as a messenger (see CCC, 329–331).

Angels are mighty beings, and their intelligence far surpasses that of human beings. We gain knowledge by the data drawn from our bodily senses. The process is gradual and involves a lot of guesswork. But the angels know in a way that is direct, immediate, essential, and unerring.

Different angels have different tasks assigned to them by

God. Some are created simply to offer worship and praise in heaven. Others have the job of assisting the Church in its prayer.

According to ancient Jewish tradition, Saint Michael is the guide and protector of God's chosen people. He was the angel sent to "go before" Israel as they journeyed to the Promised Land. He is the angelic "prince" awaited by Israel to deliver them (Daniel 12:1). Saint Jude said it was the Archangel Michael who stood guard over the body of Moses (Jude 9). The book of Revelation shows Michael commanding the armies of heaven as they conquer the forces of the devil (Revelation 12:7). As Michael had been guardian of Israel, so the early Christians viewed him as the special guardian of the Church, "the Israel of God" (Galatians 6:16).

Devotion to heaven's warrior-prince increased at the end of the nineteenth century, when Pope Leo XIII required the whole Church to recite a prescribed "Prayer to Saint Michael" at the end of every Mass:

Saint Michael the Archangel, defend us in battle;
be our protection against the wickedness and snares of the devil.
May God rebuke him, we humbly pray:
and do thou, O Prince of the heavenly host, by the power of God,
thrust into hell Satan and all the evil spirits
who prowl about the world seeking the ruin of souls. Amen.

The requirement remained in force until 1965. But the prayer itself has remained a staple of popular devotion.

The other archangels celebrated on September 29 also play prominent roles in salvation history. Saint Gabriel appears in the

Old Testament as a great messenger (see Daniel 8:16, 9:21). In the New Testament, though, he shines as the heavenly messenger who tells the Blessed Virgin Mary that she will conceive the Son of God in her womb. When we pray the "Hail Mary," we are praying the words we learned from the Archangel Gabriel: "Hail, full of grace, the Lord is with you!" (Luke 1:28).

The archangel Raphael is the heavenly spirit with the most sustained appearance in Scripture. He is a major character in the Old Testament book of Tobit. In the course of the story, he helps young Tobias find a wife—and he finds a cure for his father's blindness. So Saint Raphael is often invoked as an "angel of happy meeting" and an "angel of healing."

Devotion to the angels is something integral to the life of God's people. It is a practice that Christians and Jews have kept since ancient times, and for good reason. Angels do not move people like chess pieces. They live in relationship with us. The prophet Zechariah quizzed the angels sent to guide him. The young man Tobias spent days in conversation with his heavenly traveling companion. Saint Augustine often described our relations with the angels as "friendship." God created us to be social, and our society is both earthly and heavenly. It includes family members who look like we do, and family members who are pure spirits and have no physical appearance whatsoever. Yet they are with us, and we should acknowledge them, and we should be grateful for their help.

Jesus revealed that every human being has a guardian angel. As he spoke of little children, he said: "See that you do not despise one of these little ones; for I tell you that in heaven their angels always behold the face of my Father who is in heaven" (Matthew 18:10). In the Acts of the Apostles, we find that Saint Peter is freed from prison through the intervention of "his angel" (Acts 12:6-11). Note in both instances the use of possessive pronouns. Angels are mighty beings, powerful and intelligent, yet they do not "have" people. Rather, people have angels, by the grace of God! For that privilege the Church gives thanks and praise to God on the Memorial of the Guardian Angels.

Michaelmas is the traditional starting date for the fall semester in many European universities. Courts in the United Kingdom also begin a session on that day, and some courts in the United States have followed the custom (but without acknowledging its angelic associations). Our human knowledge and our power are pale shadows of the angels'. We do well when we depend on them, as God has ordained. We do well to celebrate their feasts!

A procession honoring the Holy Angels.

CHAPTER 19

Feasts of Churches

How lovely is thy dwelling place, O Lord of hosts!
—Psalm 84:1

IT IS A GREAT EVENT when the Church consecrates a new house
to God's service. The King of Kings reigns on earth from the
places where he is really present. God's people and angels gather
in solemn assembly where the Church celebrates the Eucharist.
The dedication of a church building is always a major event in
the history of salvation. Thus a diocese may add to its sacred calendar those days that mark the dedication of its cathedral church
or other significant local churches. Even a parish may commemorate its dedication with a special day of prayer.[1] To the local
people these are important events: God has visited his people.

Some church buildings have significance far beyond their
local congregation. There are churches whose history really belongs to the whole Church, and all of God's people mark their
dedication with feast days.

---

1 *General Instruction of the Roman Missal*, 373.

The Feast of the Dedication of Saint John Lateran, November 9, recalls the opening of the oldest of Rome's four major basilicas. In AD 324, shortly after Christianity was legalized in the Roman Empire, Pope Saint Sylvester I dedicated this church on land donated by the emperor Constantine the Great. It was called, simply, the Church of the Savior, and it served as the chief church of the Diocese of Rome. For many centuries it was the nerve center for the pope's administration, and thus for the universal Church. An inscription heralds the basilica as "the mother and the head of all of the churches of the city and the world." The dedication of the Church was later extended to Saint John the Baptist and then to Saint John the Evangelist. The word *Lateran* in the title refers to the name of the noble family who owned the land in ancient times.

The Memorial of the Dedication of the Basilicas of Saints Peter and Paul, November 18, is an optional memorial celebrating the consecration of the basilicas named for the two great men who are recognized as founders of the Roman Church. Like the Basilica of Saint John Lateran, these churches were first constructed during the reign of Constantine the Great, the first Christian emperor. The Basilica of Saint Peter has been rebuilt twice since ancient times, and the current structure is the largest and most iconic church in the world. Its grand dome is a symbol of the Church's unity and authority, and its interior houses many signs of the authority of Saint Peter, whom the Church honors as the first pope. The ancient Basilica of Saint Paul was devastated by fire in the nineteenth century and has been rebuilt according to its original plan. During the twentieth and twenty-first centuries, archaeological excavations recovered the caskets of these two apostles, both buried deep beneath the altars in their respective basilicas. Pilgrims have thronged these churches to honor the men who consecrated the empire's capital city with their blood and established Rome as the center of the Church on earth.

The Dedication of the Basilica of Saint Mary Major, August 5, is an optional memorial. It is also known as the Feast of Our Lady of Snows. According to an ancient tradition, a wealthy Christian couple in fourth-century Rome wished to build a church in honor of the Blessed Virgin. In prayer, they were led to know that snow would fall—in the hottest month of the year—and would mark off the perimeter of the church they were to build. The snow fell indeed, and it mapped out a church that is monumental. There are many great Roman churches dedicated to Mary, but the so-called "Liberian Basilica" (first built during the reign of Pope Liberius, 352–366) is the largest. The feast day commemorates the dedication of the Church after it was rebuilt in the following century, after the Council of Ephesus (AD 431) confirmed Mary's title "Mother of God."

The Feast of the Exaltation of the Holy Cross (also called the Triumph of the Cross), September 14, is a commemoration that has a rich history. It honors the cross as the instrument of salvation, and it is celebrated on the date of the dedication of the Church of the Holy

Sepulchre in Jerusalem in AD 335—the structure that includes both Jesus's tomb and the hill of Calvary, where he died. In the year 614 an army from the Sassanid Empire invaded the city, sacked the church, and confiscated a portion of the True Cross and carried it away as a trophy of the battle. The relic was recovered by the Byzantine emperor Heraclius, a Christian, in 628. Thus, the feast honors the victory of the cross for the salvation of God's people—but also the "triumph" over its captors.

On the Feast of the Exaltation of the Holy Cross,
the Church lifts high the sign and instrument of our salvation.

These are the most prominent examples of churches associated with particular feasts, but there are many others. The

Roman church of Saint Peter in Chains, for example, is usually associated with the feast of the Chair of Saint Peter, February 22. The feast commemorates the date when Saint Peter assumed his ministry of the people of Rome. The "chair" in the title refers to the bishop's *cathedra*, a traditional symbol of a bishop's authority as shepherd of the local Church. The Basilica Church of Saint Peter in Chains dates back to the fifth century and houses the chains that were used to bind Saint Peter during his imprisonments in Jerusalem and later in Rome.

CHAPTER 20

The Season of Advent

"Behold, I send my messenger before thy face,
who shall prepare thy way;
the voice of one crying in the wilderness:
Prepare the way of the Lord,
make his paths straight."
—Mark 1:2-3

ADVENT IS NOT A FEAST. It is a season. Many Christians observe it not as a time of feasting but as a time of *fasting* in expectation of the feast to come. Advent—from the Latin word *adventus,* meaning "coming"—is the name given to the weeks of preparation leading up to the Solemnity of the Nativity of the Lord: Christmas. At Christmas, the Son of God appears to the world and reveals the meaning of human history and every individual life. He answers the riddles of life and death.

In Advent the Church prepares to receive the fullness of revelation. The Scriptures proclaimed at Mass convey a sense of deep longing, but also a sure hope that God will answer the prayer of his people. During Advent the Church recalls the centuries and millennia when the world awaited the arrival of salvation. The Church remembers the oracles of the prophets of Israel, so that the world may see their fulfillment with the birth of Christ.

Yet there is another dimension to Advent. While it is about remembering the expectation of the past, it is also about intensifying the Church's expectation for the future. For Christ has promised that he will return in glory. There will be a fullness of his revelation—and the perfection of his kingdom—at the consummation of history.

At the first Christmas the Word made his dwelling among us, and he is already with us "always, to the close of the age" (Matthew 28:20). But at the close of the age "we shall see him as he is" (1 John 3:2), and God's people will share his glory. "God himself will be with them; he will wipe away every tear from their eyes, and death shall be no more, neither shall there be mourning nor crying nor pain any more" (Revelation 21:3-4).

The Church looks backward and forward during Advent, but neither dimension will distract true Christians from living in the present moment.

The story goes that one day Saint Philip Neri was shooting billiards with a group of young people, and a boy asked him what he would do if Jesus arrived right at that moment. The saint replied that he would finish the game of pool. His point was that Christians should live every minute of life in anticipation of Jesus's coming, so that they are always ready and there will be no need for rushing around.

Advent is a season of confident, peaceful waiting. There is no need for rushing around. The secular world promotes these weeks as "Christmas-shopping season," and the commercial season seems to begin earlier every year, running on an engine of anxiety. Nothing could be further from the attitude expressed by Saint Philip Neri. Nothing could be further from the spirit of anticipation taught by the prophets.

One candle of the Advent wreath is lit each Sunday
in the weeks leading up to Christmas.

Advent begins four Sundays before December 25—the Sunday that falls between November 27 and December 3 (inclusive). The Church has celebrated this season since ancient times, though the number of days has varied from time to time and from place to place. In the first millennium, Advent sometimes began on November 11, the Memorial of Saint Martin of Tours. In the Middle Ages, Advent was sometimes observed for only nine days, representing the nine months that Jesus was in Mary's womb. Many Catholics still observe those last nine days,

THE SEASON OF ADVENT

praying an "Advent Novena" (also called "Saint Andrew's Novena," since it begins on his feast day). The custom has become very popular in the pro-life movement, as it recalls the prenatal life of the Messiah, who was truly human from the moment of his conception.

Jesus has the starring role in the drama of every season of the Church's year, but his kinsman Saint John the Baptist is also prominent in Advent, especially in the Gospel selections read at Mass. John is Jesus's herald, announcing the arrival of the King, going before him to prepare the way.

The early Church learned well this season's sense of expectation. So many of the ancient liturgies echo the scriptural prayers for Christ's coming—what the Romans called his *Adventus* and the Greeks his *Parousia*. In the oldest prayers of the Mass, the people prayed "Thy kingdom come!" And they cried out in the Aramaic language spoken by Jesus and the apostles: "*Marana tha!*" Those words mean, "Come, Lord!" Saint Paul used a similar expression toward the end of his First Letter to the Corinthians. The phrase appears again, in translation, in the last lines of the Bible.

Between the first and second coming of Jesus we prepare for his final coming. In the Eastern churches, the season of Advent has a penitential character. It is a time of purification, of fasting in preparation for the feast. In the West we do not recite the "Gloria" at Mass during Advent, because that is a song proper to Christmas; it was sung by angels when Jesus was born. The song is restored at the celebration of Christ's birth, when God's glory is revealed.

The songs proper to Advent are the "O Antiphons," traditionally sung at Evening Prayer from December 1 through December 23. Most people know these prayers best from their use in the hymn "O Come, O Come, Emmanuel." These Advent songs show Christ to be the fulfillment of the longing of Israel and indeed of the whole world.

> *O come, O come, Emmanuel,*
> *and ransom captive Israel,*
> *that mourns in lonely exile here*
> *until the Son of God appear . . .*
>
> Refrain:
> *Rejoice! Rejoice! O Israel*
> *to thee shall come Emmanuel! . . .*
>
> *O come, Desire of nations, bind*
> *in one the hearts of all mankind;*
> *bid every strife and quarrel cease*
> *and fill the world with heaven's peace.*

The king has come, and his kingdom is his presence in the world. With every ordinary action of every Christian—every prayer, work, joy, and suffering—the kingdom comes. That is how we live between the first coming of Christ and the second. We live with an expectation, confidence, and joy that we magnify as a Church every Advent.

CHAPTER 21

The Fasts

"And when you fast . . ."
—Matthew 6:16

SOME OF THE CHURCH'S MOST distinctive days and seasons
are given not to feasting but to fasting. Catholics celebrate their
fasts as ardently as their feasts. We wear ashes on our forehead
on Ash Wednesday; they serve as an outward sign of our inner
poverty and hunger. Parishes draw great crowds to fish fries
on Lenten Fridays, because Catholics do not eat other meat on
those days.

To fast is to limit one's food or drink. The Church observes
many periods of fasting. Some are very brief and easy to fulfill;
the communion fast is just one hour. Some are longer and more
arduous; Ash Wednesday can seem like a long day. But the fasts
are always ordered to the feasts. They are times of purification and emptying. These observances are important, but they
are not ends in themselves. They are done for the sake of preparation. Fasts are the precondition of our being filled on the feast.

For example, we fast for one hour before receiving Jesus Christ in Holy Communion.

We abstain from meat on the Fridays of Lent, to prepare for the great feast of Easter.

For the same reason, at the beginning of Lent and at its end—on Ash Wednesday and on Good Friday—we eat only one full meal and abstain from meat. These are the only obligatory days of fasting. The United States bishops explain the Church's law: "The norms on fasting are obligatory from age 18 until age 59. When fasting, a person is permitted to eat one full meal. Two smaller meals may also be taken, but not to equal a full meal. The norms concerning abstinence from meat are binding upon members of the Latin Catholic Church from age 14 onwards."

We look to good biblical examples when we fast. Moses and Elijah fasted forty days before going into God's presence (Exodus 34:28, 1 Kings 19:8). Anna the prophetess fasted to prepare herself for the coming of the Messiah (Luke 2:37). They all wanted to see God, and they considered fasting a basic prerequisite. We, too, wish to enter God's presence, so we fast.

Jesus fasted (Matthew 4:2). Since he needed no purification, he surely did this only to set an example for us. In fact, he assumed that all Christians would follow His example. "When you fast," he said, "do not look dismal, like the hypocrites, for they disfigure their faces that their fasting may be seen by men" (Matthew 6:16). Note that he did not say "*If* you fast," but "*when.*"

Fasting has its health benefits, but it's not the same as dieting. Fasting is something spiritual and far more positive. Fasting is a spiritual feast. It does for the soul what food does for the body.

The Bible spells out specific spiritual benefits of fasting. It produces humility (Psalm 69:10). It shows our sorrow for our sins (1 Samuel 7:6). It clears a path to God (Daniel 9:3). It is a means of discerning God's will (Ezra 8:21) and a powerful method of prayer (Ezra 8:23). It is a mark of true conversion (Joel 2:12).

Fasting helps us to be detached from the things of this world. We fast not because earthly things are evil but because they're good. They're God's gifts to us. But they're so good that we sometimes prefer the gifts to the Giver. Too often we practice self-indulgence rather than self-denial. We tend to eat and drink to the point where we forget God. Such indulgence is really a form of idolatry. It's what Saint Paul meant when he said of some people that "their god is the belly, . . . with minds set on earthly things" (Philippians 3:19).

How can we enjoy God's gifts without forgetting the Giver? Fasting is a good way to start. The body wants more than it needs, so we should give it less than it wants.

Saint John of the Cross said that we cannot rise up to God if we are bound to the things of this world. When we give up good things, gradually we grow less dependent on them.

❧

Lent is the great annual season of fasting. It runs about six weeks, from Ash Wednesday to the Easter Triduum, the three days leading up to Easter. The Church treats the Triduum (Holy Thursday to Easter) and Holy Week (Palm Sunday to Easter) as distinct seasons within Lent—a time of more intensive focus on the central events of Jesus's paschal mystery.

Lent begins with the imposition of ashes,
a penitential sign, on Ash Wednesday.

In Lent the Church extends the idea of fasting beyond the
minimal skipping of meals to a more far-reaching program of
self-denial. Jesus said: "If any man would come after me, let
him deny himself . . . daily" (Luke 9:23). So Catholics "give

up" something that they'd ordinarily enjoy: sweets, soda pop, a favorite television show, or the snooze alarm.

All of this is part of our preparation for heaven; for we are destined to lose our earthly goods anyway. Time, age, illness, and "doctor's orders" can take away our taste for chocolate or our ability to enjoy a cold beer. If we have no discipline over our desires, these losses will leave us bitter and estranged from God. But if we follow Jesus in self-denial, we'll find a more habitual consolation in the ultimate good—God himself.

Nonbelievers will sometimes caricature self-denial as masochism, but this is an unjust and untrue characterization of what believers are doing. The Church has always encouraged self-control even in fasting! In the fourth century, Saint Jerome wrote: "We do not urge you to immoderate fasting or an extravagant abstinence from food. This breaks delicate frames and makes them sickly before the foundation of holy conversation is yet laid. . . . Fasting is not an absolute virtue, but the foundation of other virtues."[1]

Fasting is not the most important thing, but it is still very important. Many of the ancient Fathers held fasting to be an essential element in a Christian's life of prayer. "Repentance without fasting is useless," said Saint Basil the Great.[2] And Saint Augustine warned that to neglect the Lenten fast is sacrilege.

So Catholics have always observed fixed days of fasting. The early Christians fasted on two days every week, on Wednesday and on Friday. The Jews who were their contemporaries also fasted on two days, on Monday and on Thursday. On those days, every week, our spiritual ancestors would eat only one

---

1 Saint Jerome, Letter 130, To Demetrias, 11.

2 Saint Basil, *De ieiunio sermo* 1.3.

meal, the evening meal, and it would consist of bread and water. Many Eastern Christians have retained the ancient practice of fasting on Wednesdays and Fridays. In the West, the tradition has long been to abstain from eating meat on Fridays. For many centuries the Catholic Church prescribed meat-free Fridays, and the rule was only relaxed in the United States in the late twentieth century. Canon law still requires that Catholics observe some form of penitential discipline on all Fridays that are not solemnities.[3]

Recently the United States bishops have encouraged Catholics to take up the practice again—*voluntarily*—or at least to find some way of keeping a Friday sacrifice and offering it for a good intention. The bishops have suggested various intentions, including the end of abortion.

A regular Friday fast brings the solemn, yet joyful spirit of Lent into every week, to help us prepare for Sunday, our weekly Easter, and the great feast of the Church.

---

3 *Code of Canon Law*, 1250–1251.

CHAPTER 22

The Sacred Paschal Triduum

"The Son of man will be delivered into the hands of men,
and they will kill him; and when he is killed,
after three days he will rise."
—Mark 9:31

THE SACRED TRIDUUM IS LIKE a season within a season within a season—the concentrated center of all Christian doctrine and devotion, the paschal mystery commemorated from the moment of its inauguration at the Last Supper till the moment of its fulfillment at the Resurrection. At the end of the Church's long fast of Lent, the Triduum arrives as the dramatic climax of Holy Week.

Triduum means simply "a three-day period." These three days are Holy Thursday (also called Maundy Thursday), Good Friday, and Holy Saturday. Jesus spoke often of these days as the culmination of his saving work (see, for example, John 2:19 and Mark 10:33-34). Some scholars go so far as to say that each of the Gospels is simply the story of the Triduum with a long preface.

The Triduum is not exactly a feast, because its tone is solemn and somber. Through the liturgy and our personal prayer we are reliving the last days of Jesus's life, his betrayal and violent execution. We relive them, however, knowing that they are the price of our redemption—an astonishingly high price that he was willing to pay.

The *Catechism of the Catholic Church* calls the Triduum the source of light for the whole Church year—all the feasts—and indeed for the entire age:

> Beginning with the Easter Triduum as its source of light, the new age of the Resurrection fills the whole liturgical year with its brilliance. Gradually, on either side of this source, the year is transfigured by the liturgy. It really is a "year of the Lord's favor" (Lk 4:19). The economy of salvation is at work within the framework of time, but since its fulfillment in the Passover of Jesus and the outpouring of the Holy Spirit, the culmination of history is anticipated "as a foretaste," and the kingdom of God enters into our time. (CCC, 1168)

So, as with all of our celebrations, we remember the past and we anticipate the future.

The Triduum officially begins with the celebration of the Mass of the Lord's Supper on Holy Thursday evening. This Mass is the memorial of the institution of the Eucharist at the Last Supper, when Jesus gave his body and blood for the life of the world. Because of the greatness of this gift, the Mass is celebrated as a feast. The Church sings the "Gloria," which has been suppressed during the Lenten season. Also during the Mass it is customary for the clergy to wash the feet of some members of the congregation, in imitation of Jesus's own act of service at the Last Supper. Parishes also accompany the liturgy with special devotions honoring Jesus's eucharistic presence. There may be a procession of the Blessed Sacrament during the course of the Mass.

The blessing of palms on Palm Sunday.

After Mass on Holy Thursday, the Eucharist is traditionally exposed in the church for adoration by the people. By staying to pray, parishioners fulfill the request Jesus made to his apostles on that night, when he asked them to "watch with me one hour" while he suffered his agony (Matthew 26:40). In many places, it is customary to follow the old Roman tradition of visiting seven churches late at night on Holy Thursday, honoring Jesus present in each one.

At the Last Supper, Jesus washed the feet of his apostles.
Catholic clergy reenact the event at the Mass of the
Lord's Supper on Holy Thursday.

Earlier in the day on Holy Thursday, the bishop traditionally celebrates the annual Chrism Mass in the diocese's cathedral church, joined by many of his clergy. At the Chrism Mass
the bishop blesses the oils that will be used in the sacraments
throughout the year. The Chrism Mass also commemorates the

establishment of the sacrament of holy orders, which Jesus instituted at the Last Supper. When Jesus commanded his apostles to "do this" as his memorial sacrifice, he was commissioning them as priests. Other elements in the account of the Last Supper, such as the washing of feet, were part of the ritual ordination of priests at the Jerusalem Temple.

Carrying the cross on Good Friday.

Good Friday is dedicated to the celebration of the Lord's Passion—his suffering and death. Though there is a liturgy on that day, there is no Mass. The Church forbids the celebration of any Mass, anywhere in the world, on Good Friday. On that day we recall the way the human race responded to God's self-giving love. By our sins we still respond the way the crowds in the Gospel responded when they shouted, "Crucify him!"

Every sin is a rejection of God's love. Yet he loved us to the end, and that is what the stark Good Friday liturgy shows as it recounts the final days and hours of Jesus's life. It is a quiet ritual, with no excess. The story of the Passion is read in its entirety, with the congregation taking the part of the crowd. Petitions are raised in prayer for all the people of the world. The priest carries a cross in procession, so that it can be venerated by the people, who then come forward to kiss it. There is no Eucharistic Prayer, and no hosts are consecrated at this liturgy. After recitation of the Our Father, the priest distributes the eucharistic hosts that were consecrated the night before at the Mass of the Lord's Supper. The congregation exits the Church in silence. Parishes may also pray the Stations of the Cross earlier on Good Friday and hold Tenebrae prayer services in the evening.

On Good Friday Catholics venerate the wood of the cross,
"on which was hung our salvation."

The Church keeps Holy Saturday as a quiet day of waiting for the Lord's Resurrection. No Masses are celebrated during the daytime. The altar is left bare.

There is silence until Easter arrives in the evening at the Easter Vigil—with its light, water, songs, and sacraments.

❧

At the beginning of Holy Week, on Palm Sunday, the whole Church stands and listens to the entire passion narrative from one of the three synoptic Gospels, Matthew, Mark, or Luke. This powerful and dramatic reading is repeated again on Good Friday, when the Church proclaims Saint John's account of the suffering and death of Jesus.

Yet we do more than listen to the account of those final hours on Palm Sunday. We hold palm branches, as did the crowds that welcomed Jesus to Jerusalem that last week of his life. The palm branches symbolize our share in those events. Yet our share is more than symbolic. The events are made present to us. We, the people hailing Christ as he rides the donkey into Jerusalem, are the same people who say "Crucify him" at the end of the week, contributing to the passion and death of Christ. By our participation we acknowledge our part in the drama; by our own sins we have separated ourselves from God and required redemption. Our own sins brought about Jesus's death; and yet by his death he saves us.

The narrative of the passion and death of Jesus begins with the account of the institution of the Eucharist. All four Gospels lay special emphasis on the Last Supper, the meal where Jesus changed bread and wine into his Body and Blood. In the Gospels of Matthew, Mark, and Luke, the relationship of the Last

Supper to the events of redemption is made explicit. "Do this in memory of me," Jesus announces.

The interplay between ritual and history that took place in the Exodus is repeated in the passion, death, and resurrection of Christ. In commanding the Church to repeat his sacrificial offering as a "memorial" to him, he established the Last Supper as the ceremonial setting for the re-presentation of the events of our salvation. In this memorial sacrifice, the new covenant is constantly renewed with every succeeding generation.

Unlike any other form of remembrance, the Mass, thanks to God's gracious gift, the outpouring of the Holy Spirit, has the power to make present the very reality it symbolizes.

During Holy Week and the sacred Triduum, the Church, as she has done for over twenty centuries, calls Christians not just to *commemorate* events of long ago, but also to *enter* the mystery today. We are not bystanders. We have been invited to be participants in the mystery of our redemption.

CHAPTER 23

Today

"Today, when you hear his voice,
do not harden your hearts."
—Hebrews 3:7-8

SOME DAYS ARE DRAMATIC by their very nature. When we gather for a baptism, a wedding, a funeral, an ordination, or a retirement, we mark a transition in life, a movement from one stage to another, a fundamental change in circumstance. Our feelings are complex, and from moment to moment they may shift from wistfulness to fear, awe to giddiness. It's all the matter of a single day—though the vigil, the preparation, has its own drama.

Most days do not seem so momentous. Nor do they have the obvious significance of a wedding anniversary or the due date for the taxes. Yet these are the days that make up the majority of our lives. These are the days for which we'll be judged: the hundreds of days per year that are quite ordinary. Not every game clinches a pennant, but every game counts on the way to the clincher; and the happiest players on the field are those who keep a lively awareness of the value of every game.

The feasts of the year belong to those who are faithful. As the Jewish philosopher Philo showed us, people who
keep the law live in a perpetual feast. Philo's early-Christian
countryman Origen of Alexandria concurred, adding that,
when Christians are devout, "all [their] days are the Lord's,
and [they are] always keeping the Lord's day."[1] A twentieth-
century churchman, Cardinal Jean Danielou, expanded on
Origen's observation:

> Their life is thus a perpetual feast-day. And this contem-
> plative life, at once that of the patriarchs and that of Chris-
> tians, is the image, the *eikon* of the "blessed rest," that of
> heaven, where, freed from all servitude one can contem-
> plate intelligible realities. The Sabbath itself was intro-
> duced by the law of Moses because of the people (*plethos*),
> as an educational means to lead them to the more perfect
> practice of the perpetual and spiritual Sabbath.[2]

The calendar is a teacher, a catechist, a trainer. The feasts
are rehearsals for daily living in the kingdom of heaven. But
we gain that kingdom later by living it now. The kingdom is
already among us and within us (Luke 17:21), wherever Christ
reigns. In our many feasts we acknowledge his reign, and we
extend it to our every day.

The Church spends thirty-three weeks every year in the
season we call "Ordinary Time." We call it "ordinary" simply
because its weeks are ordered; they are numbered in order. The
Latin term for the season is *tempus per annum* (literally "time

---

1 A paraphrasing of Origen, *Contra Celsum* 8.22.
2 Jean Danielou, *The Bible and the Liturgy* (Notre Dame, Ind.: University of Notre Dame
Press, 1956), 247.

during the year"). What workaday names we apply to days that are brimful of glory. Yet such is the condition of the world since the incarnation of God's Son. Jesus Christ now dwells among us, even in the most ordinary circumstances.

Ordinary Time unfolds in two periods during the year. The first period starts the day after the Feast of the Baptism of the Lord (at the end of Christmas Season) and ends the day before Ash Wednesday. The second period begins on the Monday after Pentecost (at the end of Easter Season) and ends the Saturday before the First Sunday of Advent.

Ordinary Time has no special customs associated with it— no baskets of candy, no ornaments on trees, no ashes on foreheads. Yet for the believer it is a feast of the spirit, because God has entered history as an ordinary laborer and family man in a sleepy town of no importance. The Word was made flesh and dwells among us, and the fact itself is a feast.

An important part of the original mission of Christianity was to teach the world how to feast—how to celebrate good things, and how to use the goods of the world in celebration. It was not an easy adjustment for the pagan world, and Saint Paul's letters show the strain of one man's efforts to teach former pagans the Jewish tradition of the sacred banquet, with all its joy and all its solemnity. Table manners arise as a major theme in the apostle's three most important letters: Romans, Galatians, and First Corinthians.

He had heard that Christians were getting drunk, eating like gluttons, and neglecting the poor who were at table with them. Their celebration led not to communion and fellowship but to division and exclusion.

When you meet together, it is not the Lord's supper that you eat. For in eating, each one goes ahead with his own meal, and one is hungry and another is drunk. What! Do you not have houses to eat and drink in? Or do you despise the church of God and humiliate those who have nothing? What shall I say to you? Shall I commend you in this? No, I will not.

For I received from the Lord what I also delivered to you, that the Lord Jesus on the night when he was betrayed took bread, and when he had given thanks, he broke it, and said, "This is my body which is for you. Do this in remembrance of me." In the same way also the cup, after supper, saying, "This cup is the new covenant in my blood.

Do this, as often as you drink it, in remembrance of me." For as often as you eat this bread and drink the cup, you proclaim the Lord's death until he comes.

Whoever, therefore, eats the bread or drinks the cup of the Lord in an unworthy manner will be guilty of profaning the body and blood of the Lord. . . .

So then, my brethren, when you come together to eat, wait for one another—if any one is hungry, let him eat at home—lest you come together to be condemned. (1 Corinthians 11:20-27, 33)

It was as if the world needed basic instruction in happiness. It was as if humankind would choose misery unless God commanded them to do otherwise.

Indeed, Jesus was not a man who multiplied commandments. He preferred that people learn from him (see Matthew 11:29) and imitate him out of love rather than fear. But at the most dramatic moment in his earthly life he issued a command in no uncertain terms. He ordered his disciples to keep the feast of his memorial: *"Do this in remembrance of me"* (Luke 22:19).

So "this" is what the Church does as it keeps the *perpetual* feast of Jesus Christ, and the special feasts of the Christian calendar.

The need for Christ's feast in a post-Christian world is little different from that of a pre-Christian world. We live among people—even Christians!—who, week after week, are working for the weekend, yet they never enter God's rest. They know oblivion and escape but never inner peace.

Christ came that we might have abundant life (see John 10:10), and that is what he dispenses through the feasts of his Church.

We need, once again, to teach the world how to celebrate, how to feast, how to be happy.

☙❧

In teaching the world to feast, we will introduce the world, once again, to Jesus Christ. The *Catechism* tells us: "'All that Jesus did and taught, from the beginning until the day when he was taken up to heaven' (Acts 1:1-2), is to be seen in the light of the mysteries of Christmas and Easter" (CCC, 512).

The feasts bring Christ to everyone, and our celebrations ensure that even the poorest people enjoy a day of rest and favor. The feasts are deeply democratic institutions, because all

Christ's riches are intended "for every individual and are everybody's property."[3]

Feasts represent the public face of the joy of Christianity. They are tremendously attractive—and, for that very reason they will frighten some people.

In seventeenth-century England, the Puritan-led government issued a ban on Christmas. Parliament judged celebrations to be a waste of time—time that could be productively spent at work. They went so far as to declare December 25 a national day of fasting.

It didn't work. Christmas won, and the day came back more festive than ever.

The seventeenth-century Puritans may seem amusing to us now, but they represent an anti-Catholic, anti-*festive* spirit that is always in the world. When Pope Gregory reformed the calendar, drawing from the work of the best scientists in his day, a great number of non-Catholic countries refused to adopt his calendar. The Protestant astronomer Johannes Kepler joked that some people would rather disagree with the sun than agree with the pope.

Today's Puritans tend to have a secularist bent, but they are as joyless as their spiritual ancestors. They would rather drain the cheer out of days than permit any public reference to Jesus Christ. They advocate legislation to have his name and symbols removed from every postage stamp, courthouse square, and even window sills that can be seen from the street.

We should charitably resist their efforts. We should, by the example of our joy, teach the world how to feast.

---

3 Pope John Paul II, *Redemptor Hominis* (encyclical), March 4, 1979, 11.

☙☙

Even as we teach, we will be learning. Saint Faustina Kowal-ska, the nun who inspired the annual feast of Divine Mercy, was pleased to learn her Christianity from the unfolding of the Church year. She wrote: "Almost every feast of the Church gives me a deeper knowledge of God and a special grace. That is why I prepare myself for each feast and unite myself closely with the spirit of the Church."[4]

The feasts seem to be a crazy quilt of customs, but they are lessons, too. They teach us. They evangelize us. They are our dress rehearsal for heaven. They tell and retell the story of the Gospel. They proclaim the dogmas of the faith. But they do all this in the sweetest and most memorable way—in a family way. In the words of Pope Francis: "The Church, like every family, passes on to her children the whole store of her memories. But how does this come about in a way that nothing is lost, but rather everything in the patrimony of faith comes to be more deeply understood? It is through the apostolic Tradition pre-served in the Church with the assistance of the Holy Spirit."[5]

The feasts are days set apart, but they give life to the whole of the year. As the philosopher Josef Pieper demonstrated: to celebrate at all is to celebrate it all. Saint Paul said: "We know that in everything God works for good with those who love him" (Romans 8:28). We can celebrate even in the midst of ter-rors and trials. On the great vigil of the greatest feast of the year, we manage even to celebrate the fact of our original sin! "O happy fault that earned for us so great, so glorious a Redeemer!"

---

4 Saint Faustina Kowalska, *Diary,* 481.

5 Pope Francis, *Lumen Fidei* (encyclical), June 29, 2013, 40.

It is the life of the glorious Redeemer the people of the earth receive again and again in the feasts of the Church. "The liturgical year," said Pope Pius XII, "is not a cold and lifeless representation of the events of the past, or a simple and bare record of a former age. It is rather Christ himself who is ever living in His Church."[6]

---

6 Pope Pius XII, *Mediator Dei* (encyclical on the Sacred Liturgy), November 9, 1947, 165.

For Further Reading

Documents of the Church

All are available online at the websites of the Vatican (www.Vatican.va) *and the United States Conference of Catholic Bishops* (www.USCCB.org).

General Instruction of the Roman Missal (with adaptations for dioceses in the United States of America). Congregation for Divine Worship and the Discipline of the Sacraments. English translation by International Committee on English in the Liturgy Corporation. Published by the United States Conference of Catholic Bishops, 2011.

General Norms for the Liturgical Year and the Calendar. Vatican Congregation for Divine Worship. February 14, 1969.

Directory on Popular Piety and the Liturgy. Vatican Congregation for Divine Worship and the Discipline of the Sacraments. December 2001. (See especially Chapter 4, "The Liturgical Year and Popular Piety.")

Catechism of the Catholic Church. 2nd ed. Washington, D.C.: USCCB, 1997. (See especially CCC 1163–1173, 2168–2195.)

Code of Canon Law. 1983. (See especially 1244–1258 on Sacred Times.)

Sacrosanctum Concilium (Constitution on the Sacred Liturgy). Second Vatican Council. December 4, 1963.

Martyrologium Romanum. Congregation for Divine Worship and the Discipline of the Sacraments. Rome: Libreria Editrice Vaticana, 2004. (There is no English translation.)

Liturgical Calendar for the Dioceses of the United States of America. Committee on Divine Worship. Washington, D.C.: USCCB. (This resource is updated yearly.)

Pope Paul VI, *Mysterii Paschalis* (*Motu proprio* on the Liturgical Year and the New Universal Roman Calendar). February 14, 1969.

By the Authors of This Book

CARDINAL DONALD WUERL AND MIKE AQUILINA

The Mass: The Glory, the Mystery, the Tradition. New York: Image, 2011.

The Church: Unlocking the Secrets to the Places Catholics Call Home. New York: Image, 2012.

CARDINAL DONALD WUERL

Faith That Transforms Us: Reflections on the Creed. Frederick, MD: Word Among Us, 2013.

Seek First the Kingdom: Challenging the Culture by Living Our Faith. Huntington, Ind.: Our Sunday Visitor, 2012.

The Catholic Way: Faith for Living Today. New York: Doubleday, 2001.

The Teaching of Christ: A Catholic Catechism for Adults. Coeditor with Father Ronald Lawler, Thomas Comerford Lawler, and Father Kris Stubna. Huntington, Ind.: Our Sunday Visitor, 2004.

The Gift of Faith: A Question and Answer Catechism. Coeditor with Father Ronald Lawler and Thomas Comerford Lawler. Huntington, Ind.: Our Sunday Visitor, 2001.

The Catholic Priesthood Today. Chicago: Franciscan Herald Press, 1976.

Fathers of the Church. Boston, Mass.: St. Paul Editions, 1986.

MIKE AQUILINA

A Year with the Angels. Charlotte, NC: Saint Benedict Press, 2011.

A Year with the Church Fathers: Patristic Wisdom for Daily Living. Charlotte, NC: Saint Benedict Press, 2010.

Roots of the Faith: From the Church Fathers to You. Ann Arbor, Mich.: Servant Books, 2010.

Praying the Psalms with the Early Christians: Ancient Songs for Modern Hearts. Coauthor with Christopher Bailey. Ijamsville, MD: Word Among Us, 2009.

Signs and Mysteries: Revealing Ancient Christian Symbols. Co-author with Lea Marie Ravotti. Huntington, Ind.: Our Sunday Visitor, 2008.

The Mass of the Early Christians. Huntington, Ind.: Our Sunday Visitor, 2001.

What Catholics Believe: A Pocket Catechism. Coauthor with Father Kris D. Stubna. Huntington, Ind.: Our Sunday Visitor, 1999.